THE SWORD
AND THE WARRIOR WAITING
ON
FIRE

PAUL D CARROLL

WESTBOW
PRESS®
A DIVISION OF THOMAS NELSON
& ZONDERVAN

WestBow Press books may be ordered through booksellers or by contacting:

WestBow Press
A Division of Thomas Nelson & Zondervan
1663 Liberty Drive
Bloomington, IN 47403
www.westbowpress.com
844-714-3454

ISBN: 979-8-3850-4347-7 (sc)
ISBN: 979-8-3850-4348-4 (e)

Library of Congress Control Number: 2025902251

Print information available on the last page.

WestBow Press rev. date: 02/19/2025

About the cover image:

Church of the Holy Sepulcher, crosses engraved by crusader soldiers and pilgrims on the stone walls of the church.

Do we ever get burdened and tired by the way we think, or how we may perceive our self-identity? Tired of the grind? Good news! There is daily hope!

Romans 12:2 (NLT) "...., but let God TRANSFORM you into a NEW PERSON by CHANGING the way you THINK."

God still speaks TODAY. God still speaks to his children today if we allow Him and expect Him to speak to us. This takes us on a journey that pierces the darkness of our mental and spiritual daily struggles and leads us into the presence of God's Kingdom. In God's Kingdom there is soul altering freedom. God has opened the door to us into His presence daily. We are invited to enter in and pick up His Two-Edged Sword and wield it. First, we are to receive from the abundant riches of His Spirit, and secondly, to therefore, give unto others what he has given to us. This is our lifeline, our battle and freedom. We are called to ask, listen, receive, speak and act, functioning in, not the world's, but His, new every day, miraculous and all-powerful KINGDOM NOW, TODAY! When God speaks to us, all becomes new, even the way we think. We become filled with His hope, love, peace and power, taking this daily with us where ever we may go. We are divinely changed by His Word!

1

Words that SPEAK into our life's situations today. WORDS that go deep into our soul and speak light and 'wake up' calls to our minds.

1 Thessalonians 5 (NLT)," Always be joyful. Never stop praying. Be thankful in all circumstances, for this is God's will for you who belong to Christ Jesus. "

And here are beautiful words from the NLT Life Application Study Bible to the above verse "Our joy, prayers, and thankfulness should not fluctuate with our circumstances or feelings. Obeying these three commands--BE JOYFUL, NEVER stop PRAYING and BE THANKFUL-- often goes against our natural inclinations. When we make a conscious decision to do what God says, however, we will begin to see people in a new perspective. When we do God's will, we will find it easier to be joyful and thankful." So, going into work today, facing any of life's blessings, or challenges, this is how we must enter the ring. JOYFUL! THANKFUL! ALWAYS PRAYING!

_____

_____

_____

_____

_____

_____

_____

_____

_____

2

I feel God saying, "I am not calling you to live in a world of comfort. I am calling you to live in a world of sacrifice." Mark 8:34 (Berean Study Bible) "Then Jesus called the crowd to him along with his disciples and he told them, "if anyone wants to come after me, he must deny himself and take up his cross and follow me. " The life of, 'oh I am cozy. I am comfortable. I've got it made. Me and my comfy slippers.' We can live in a false world of comfort while our spiritual strength and the impact we are supposed to be having upon the world and others is being dissipated. again, I feel God saying "I am not calling you to live in a world of comfort. I am calling you to live in a world of sacrifice."

_____

_____

_____

_____

_____

_____

_____

_____

_____

_____

_____

3

Jesus says, "This is my commandment: Love each other in the same way I have loved you." John 15:12 (NLT). Really!? No matter how hard I try this human will fall short. But, what Jesus said is not a suggestion. It is a command! To do this I must go beyond my own human experience. I must go out of this world. I must have a new Spirit put on like putting on new clothing. I must wear something greater than myself. The Holy Spirit. I am not called to just believe in Him, but to wear Him!

Galatians 4:6 (NIV)

Because you are his sons, God sent the Spirit of his Son into our hearts, the Spirit who calls out, "Abba, Father."

_____

_____

_____

_____

_____

_____

_____

_____

_____

_____

_____

_____

4

Beautiful words of encouragement for life today in the midst of the challenging times we live in! Who can change our world? We can! We can as we act with boldness in knowing who we are ACTING on behalf of. We are all called to be Esther's and Mordechai's in our worlds. Do you still have breath? Don't give up! New Living Testament notes on Esther 10:3

"in the Book of Esther, we clearly see God at work in the lives of individuals and in the Affairs of a Nation. Even when it looks as if the world is in the hands of evil people, God is still in control, protecting those who are his. Although we may not understand everything happening around us, we must trust in God's protection and retain our integrity by doing what we know is right. Esther, who risked her life by appearing before the king, became a heroine. Mordecai, who is effectively condemned to death, Rose to become the second highest ranking official in the nation. No matter how hopeless our condition, or how much we would like to give up, we need not despair. God is in control of our world."

_____

_____

_____

_____

_____

_____

_____

_____

_____

_____

5

Merriam-Webster definition of GRACE.

grace (Entry 1 of 2)

1a: unmerited divine assistance given to humans for their regeneration or sanctification

b: a virtue coming from God

c: a state of sanctification enjoyed through divine assistance

Sanctification, holiness, can be "enjoyed" experienced, worn, put on today. We may feel sanctification is a goal we cannot receive and therefore we may fear doom awaiting us. But in reality, it is not so. Sanctification is my gift, free, from God. Received today because of what Jesus did yesterday when He died on the cross; for me. So, I can "enjoy" it today.

From Revelations last chapter. Chapter 22. (BSB)

"The Spirit and the bride say "Come." Let anyone who hears this say, "Come." Let anyone who is thirsty come. Let anyone who desires drink freely from the Water of Life."

So, let us "Come." and say, "Come."

The last sentence in Revelation 22:21 (BSB) says, "The grace of the Lord Jesus be with all the saints.Amen."

"May the grace of the Lord Jesus be with God's holy people." It is offered to us today. It is done. It is finished. Ask.

_____

_____

_____

_____

_____

6

Let us focus on the one thing that holds ALL POWER, not our fancy worded prayers, or the current 'pop' Christian phrases or words we use today to show we are connected to God. 1 Corinthians 1:17 (NLT) "For Christ didn't send me to baptize, but to preach the good news, and not with clever speech, for fear that the CROSS OF CHRIST would lose its power. The message of the Cross is foolish to those who are headed for Destruction! But we who are being saved know it is a very POWER OF GOD."

_____

_____

_____

_____

_____

_____

_____

_____

_____

_____

_____

_____

7

FASTING is not a time of suffering. It is a time of victory and joy. He said to them, Mark 2:29 (NKJV) "This kind can come out by nothing but prayer and fasting."

What an awesome supernatural gift God has given us in prayer and FASTING. Do you want to release others and yourself into living in God's accord, chains snapped, healings happening, freedom achieved? We are to be 'dead to this world' but alive in Christ. Prayer and FASTING is a joyful, victorious gift. In our modern age, how often do we use this gift?

_____

_____

_____

_____

_____

_____

_____

_____

_____

_____

_____

_____

_____

_____

8

Yes, we live in woeful times where those in power and the masses seem to call the good 'evil' and the evil 'good'. We see a move towards a world govt that is bent on taking away freedoms and making us all their slaves. However, God is still sovereign! In 2 Chronicles 35 God spoke to the pagan king Neco, and the king even messaged the king of Israel, that God spoke to him. Yes, God spoke to and led the king of a pagan nation to accomplish His purposes. We live in daunting times, but is not, our sovereign God, using this for His purposes still? What could be His purpose? He is coming! Could one thing be that He is GETTING US, INDIVIDUALLY, AND THE CHURCH READY FOR HIS COMING? A glorious day is coming! I believe He is making us READY.

_____

_____

_____

_____

_____

_____

_____

_____

_____

_____

_____

_____

_____

9

EYES ON JESUS. How do we get through these difficult times? The natural thing to do is worry. As Christians, we are called to live in the Supernatural realm. We live in a new reality by keeping our eyes on Jesus. Peter, walking on water, took his eyes off Jesus and started to focus on the storm around him and the natural overcame him. He sank. Hebrews 12:1,2 (NLT) says, " and let us run with endurance the race God has set before us. We do this by keeping our eyes on Jesus, the champion who initiates and perfects our faith." Through these difficult times, we are called by God to walk in the Supernatural because of who He is, and because He is with us! We overcome by KEEPING OUR EYES ON JESUS!

_____

_____

_____

_____

_____

_____

_____

_____

_____

_____

_____

_____

10

The Head. Control the head and you control them. "And I will cause hostility between you and the woman, and between your offspring and her offspring. He will strike your head, and you will strike his heel." Genesis 3:15 (NLT) In football, when I was playing inside linebacker, I would have offensive lineman, much bigger than myself, powering off the line to crush and take me out of the play. Seemingly, my survival, would be to avoid them, go around them or do a quick matador 'Ole!'. But no, I went through them! I stopped them in their tracks and threw them aside. I was able to move a bigger body by controlling their head. No matter how big you are your body will go with the head. Control the head, you control the whole body. So, my focus was to, with a powerful blow, put my helmet into the center of their helmet, controlling their advance, which would block the line for the running back to get through, and then tossing them out of the way and, myself, or another defensive player, would tackle the running back. The key was the HEAD. No matter how big and strong they were, the head always controls you, and where their head goes they went. We have an enemy in this life, Satan, and he wants to control your head, to get into the way you THINK and influence and try to control you. The mind is a battlefield. How we think is so critical, but Jesus has already delivered that victorious blow to the enemy. We just need to take ahold of it. Romans 12:2 (NLT) "Don't copy the behavior and customs of this world, but let God transform you into a new person by changing the way you think." Concerning control, our direction daily, it's about the HEAD, the mind, the way you think. Now we have to let God control and change the direction of the way we think. Ask Him, and He will. Get into His Living Word and He will speak to you. His Words to you will change you, the way you think. He is there with you, wanting to, offering you this gift. So, allow Him to 'change you, even the way you think'. Peace.

_____

_____

_____

11

2 Cor 1:8-10 (NLT) "We were crushed and overwhelmed beyond our ability to endure, and we thought we would never live through it. In fact, we expected to die. But as a result, we stopped relying on ourselves and learned to rely only on God, who raises the dead. And he did rescue us from mortal danger, and he will rescue us again. We have placed our confidence in him, and he will continue to rescue us."

Painful trials in life seem so hard to endure but we must learn to grasp them in thankfulness because when we go through them we see God used them, not to destroy us, but rather to give us a greater victory of strength, power, love and sound mind. To be made more into the image of Jesus is greater than all else in this world. Learning to rely not upon our own strength but upon His presence with us. He always shows up. This is our expectation of faith; to expect Him to do something great in our lives today.

_____

_____

_____

_____

_____

_____

_____

_____

_____

_____

_____

ISAIAH 40:31 (NIV)

31 "but those who HOPE in the Lord will renew their strength. They will soar on wings like eagles; they will run and not grow weary, they will walk and not be faint."

What a powerful and beautiful scripture to be chewed on. HOPE! Where is our daily hope? Do we put all the weight upon something to change, or become better, in this life, to make us feel good about ourselves? Is our hope in money, fame, job, career, spouse, recognition, relationship, weather (you'll understand this one if you are from Seattle, WA state area), politics, or any of the other things that can replace our hope in God? If our life's situations, or our self-identity and thoughts, are not feeling right today, how are we looking for a change to come? What will make us feel better? God tells us to HOPE in him. When we do, what happens to us is in Isaiah 4:31.

Jesus blessings and divine protection on us today.

_____

_____

_____

_____

_____

_____

_____

_____

13

EXPECT God's intervention! Walk above the norm today. We can take part in God's miraculous. Jesus is walking by us on the water today as He did by the disciple's boat. Walking on water is not normal. This is the Divine miraculous. In the midst of the storm Peter, the only one on the ship who asks, asks Jesus, "If it is really you, tell me to come to you, walking on the water." Matt 14:28 (NLT) Jesus response to him, and to us today as we go through our various storms, is "Yes, come." Sometimes, we have not because we don't ask. He is calling us to join Him in His supernatural realities. We are not called to live by any worldly fear.

14

Braveheart "FREEDOM!!!!!!!"

God's Word is freedom. It is worth even more passion!

Psalm 119:45 (NIV)

"I will walk about in freedom, for I have sought out your precepts."

_____

_____

_____

_____

_____

_____

_____

_____

_____

_____

_____

_____

_____

_____

_____

_____

15

Through what I experience today. How am I to be? How am I to respond to others and life's situations? Don't you love Gods Word? It is a light to our path.

1Cor 16:13,14 (NLT)

"BE ON GUARD. STAND FIRM IN THE FAITH. BE COURAGEOUS. BE STRONG. AND DO EVERYTHING WITH LOVE."

_____

_____

_____

_____

_____

_____

_____

_____

_____

_____

_____

_____

_____

_____

16

Wouldnt it be great if we could go through this whole day today with CONFIDENCE. Confidence in what? Confidence in our SALVATION! Thess 5:8 (NLT) "....and wearing as our helmet the CONFIDENCE of our SALVATION." God's Word refers to us and calls us to carry our sword, our shield, our helmet. Why? Because we ARE WARRIORS! If you want to pierce whatever darkness sorrounds you today than put on the confidence of your salvation. Regardless of what we may face today KNOW, and carry the hope, that we will see that glorious day when we will be, "caught up in the clouds to meet the Lord in the air." So, carry the CONFIDENCE of your SALVATION into whatever situations we may face today and pierce the darkness.

_____

_____

_____

_____

_____

_____

_____

_____

_____

_____

_____

_____

Take heart if you are going through trials. You're GOD'S CHILD! Like a good father would do, He disciplines His children. So, we can really take solace and be thankful when God is disciplining us. God is not with us just to make our lives a Disneyland. He is making us into the IMAGE of His SON, JESUS. "Endure God's loving discipline."

Hebrews 12:5-7 (NLT)

"and have you forgotten the encouraging words God spoke to you as his children? He said, 'My child, don't make light of the Lord's discipline, and don't give up when he corrects you. For the Lord disciplines those he loves, and he punishes each one he accepts as his child.' As you endure this Divine discipline, remember that God is treating you as his own children...." Getting punished, being disciplined, doesn't sound so inviting. Wouldn't we much rather here the message that God is going to give us more money, luxury cars, bigger houses, and all the good stuff? But, God's ultimate divine goal, for us, becoming more like Jesus, is more than worth it all. Let's keep our eyes on the champion Jesus.

_____

_____

_____

_____

_____

_____

_____

_____

_____

18

WE PUT OUR LIVES INTO THE DIVINE HANDS OF OUR
LOVING FATHER IN HEAVEN. HIS PLANS AND WILL BE DONE
IN OUR LIFE TODAY. GOD IS GOOD TO, SORROUNDS, AND
TAKES SPECIAL CARE OF HIS CHILDREN!!!

_____

_____

_____

_____

_____

_____

_____

_____

_____

_____

_____

_____

_____

_____

_____

19

Feel like evil is getting out of CONTROL, and TAKING control, trying to rule you, throughout this world? We have the power hungry trying to remove God and sit on His throne.

Revelation 22;12,13 (NLT)

"Look, I am coming soon, bringing my reward with me to repay all people as according to their deeds. I am the Alpha and the Omega, the First and the Last, the Beginning and the End."

Who rules? GOD RULES! Our God is sovereign! As His children, we are in a good place. He is with us.

Let us listen to our DADDY in heaven and boldly go do His work today! Love one another as Jesus loves us.

_____

_____

_____

_____

_____

_____

_____

_____

_____

_____

20

Then Jesus said, "Come to me, all of you who are weary and carry heavy burdens, and I will give you rest. Take my yoke upon you. Let me teach you, because I am humble and gentle at heart and you will find rest for your souls. For my yoke is easy to bear, and the burden I give you is light. " Matt 11:28 (NLT)

I believe that in these times, of now, Jesus is pouring out His Holy Spirit more abundantly. He is calling us to walk in the SUPERNATURAL more and more. I feel He is also giving His children a reminder as we walk into these supernatural times. That even, more importantly, He is calling us to walk in His Supernatural CHARACTER as well. In the above scripture, Jesus says He is humble and gentle at heart. We are to receive His character as well too! Jesus said, John 13:34 (NLT) "I give you a new commandment, that you love one another as I loved you." Yes, there is power in Jesus name. We can walk around with this power, but never know Jesus. The Holy Spirit gives POWER, LOVE, and a SOUND MIND, not just power. The Holy Spirit is now molding us into the image of Jesus. As we enter these miraculous and powerful times to be a Christian, let us not forget to allow this SPIRIT to change our characters as well.

_____

_____

_____

_____

_____

_____

_____

21

The world and WORLD GOVT are trying to make us all FEARFUL SLAVES. What do you WANT though!!? You can have it!

Romans 8:15-17 (NLT)

"So, you have not received a spirit that makes you fearful slaves. Instead, you received God's Spirit when he adopted you as his own children. Now we call him, "Abba, Father." for His Spirit joins with our spirit to affirm that we are God's children. And since we are his children, we are his heirs. In fact, together with Christ we are Heirs of God's glory. But if we are to share his glory, we must also share his suffering."

_____

_____

_____

_____

_____

_____

_____

_____

_____

_____

_____

_____

_____

22

Rom 8:27

"........, for the Spirit PLEADS for us believers in harmony with God's own will."

PLEAD means to argue a case, or cause, in a court or to appeal earnestly; beg. We may not realize it, but, we have the divine, the Holy Spirit, actually pleading for us. He sees us as we are before God, His finished and complete child, not just the one who denies Him 3 times, or the one who takes our eyes off Him and then sinks in the water. Even when we are not aware of it, the Holy Spirit is pleading for us. We have this divine covering. God is all in for His children! Thanks, and praise for our loving Father.

_____

_____

_____

_____

_____

_____

_____

_____

_____

_____

_____

_____

23

For a while, let's let go off our effort to achieve HOLINESS, our internal struggle, and receive God's message that we are holy. The good news is, 'HE DID IT, not us! When HE calls us holy, we are holy!

We don't have to go work for it to get it today. We already have it! Let's receive this and let our minds and souls rest.

1 Corinthians 1:2

"He made you holy by means of Christ Jesus, just as He did for all people everywhere who call on the name of our Lord Jesus Christ, their Lord and ours."

_____

_____

_____

_____

_____

_____

_____

_____

_____

_____

_____

_____

_____

WOW!!!! You could even say this is God's message to US, the CHURCH, today. It is simple but so powerful. It is like a 'Drop the Mike' word. 1 John 2:6 (NLT)"THOSE WHO SAY THEY LIVE IN GOD SHOULD LIVE THEIR LIVES AS JESUS DID." We are all called to not just believe in Jesus, but to actually LIVE Jesus! LOVE UP! POWER UP! ACTION UP!

_____

_____

_____

_____

_____

_____

_____

_____

_____

_____

_____

_____

_____

_____

_____

PLEASE let us not think we are small today and can have little to no impact on our world around us. God has made us powerful!

Revelation 1:5,6 (NLT)

"All glory to him who loves us and has freed us from our sins by shedding his blood for us, he has made us a kingdom of PRIESTS for God his father. All glory and power to him forever and ever! Amen."

Where do we sit today? Where do we stand today? What life situations do we find ourselves in? No matter, let our souls and spirits rise today for we are chosen priests of our God!

_____

_____

_____

_____

_____

_____

_____

_____

_____

_____

_____

_____

_____

26

Sorry, Christian brothers and sisters, it is good to know the truth. We LIVE in an EVIL WORLD, and sounds like, according to God's Word, it is not going to change until Jesus comes back. So, lets prepare ourselves for the work ahead. However, it will change on that Titus 2:13 (NLT) "wonderful day when the glory of our great God and Savior, Jesus Christ, will be revealed." To face reality is a good thing. We can face reality and learn how to live powerfully within it. In Titus it says Titus 2:12 (NLT)"We should live within this EVIL world with wisdom, righteousness, and devotion to God." We can have a changing effect upon our own worlds of connections, but this WORLD we live in will remain evil until Jesus comes back. So, how are we to walk in it? Titus 2:12-14 (NLT)"And we are instructed to turn from Godless living and sinful pleasures. We should live in this evil world with wisdom, righteousness, and Devotion to God, while we look forward with hope to that wonderful day when the glory of our great God and savior, Jesus Christ, will be revealed. He gave his life to free us from every kind of sin, to cleanse us, and to make us his very own people, totally committed to doing good deeds."

_____

_____

_____

_____

_____

_____

_____

_____

_____

27

Transformation. The Lord's prayer. If Jesus told us this is how we are to pray, then why do we mentally push this aside as merely a verbal ritual of recitation? It is the most beautiful, ingenious and powerful prayer to pray! Matt 6:9 (KJB)"Our FATHER which art in heaven". Jesus tells us to commune with, talk with, not just an almighty powerful being, yes that is true, but it is a Being that loves us as a good father. He says KNOW Him! Come and talk with Him! Be with Him! He loves you. Then it says, Matt 6:10 (KJB) "Thy kingdom come. Thy will be done ON EARTH AS IT IS IN HEAVEN." Itis saying that not my own desires be done, but with faith and trust that His Divine, knows better than me, and when I ASK I can trust in my good Father that He has heard and His divine will, WILL be done in any situation. The desire of the Father is that we commune with Him. And, it is saying that we CAN have His divine loving presence with us. How would you like to walk through the day and be attacked by this or that evil and just be able to say "no" to it, submit it to your Heavenly Father who is watching and listening and then put it in His hands because you trust and know His will, not the enemies, will be done on earth as it is in heaven? And, our God has a good will for us. Submitted to God, as such, the devil flees. PEACE!

28

Let us not forget the glory and authority of whose name we are using when we pray, "In Jesus name." Sometimes, as humans, we can mentally reduce it to just another word formula used to get our prayer heard and answered. It is so much more! We are communicating with the creator of all things! The exact likeness of God! The glory of God that is seen in the face of Jesus Christ! Words from 2 Cor 4:7 (NLT), " we now have this light shining in our hearts, but we ourselves are like fragile clay jars containing this great treasure. This makes it clear that OUR GREAT POWER is from God, not from ourselves." We have GREAT POWER, but it is not from ourselves. It is from our Almighty Jesus, whose name we use. When God's Word says you have great power, do not choose to believe different. We are to arise as a powerful body of Christ, not just the heads of, or the hands of the church, no, the whole church! Do not believe the father of all lies, believe Your Father! And, He says you are powerful because of the NAME of who is with you. In the NAME of Jesus......

_____

_____

_____

_____

_____

_____

_____

_____

_____

_____

29

If for some reason today, I was dying and on my last breaths, I wouldn't be thinking, 'I'm sure glad I just had that Taco Bell Super Mex burrito. Man, was it delicious!' Or, any other material thoughts, but, one thing I would be thinking, 'Father God, I am so glad I know You as a friend!' So, what do we pursue today? Let's be thankful that God has given us eternity.

_____

_____

_____

_____

_____

_____

_____

_____

_____

_____

_____

_____

_____

_____

_____

_____

This is IT! Everything we have. Everything we hope for. Our true freedom. Our past, our present, our futures. Why we live and have existence. Why we have breath today!

1 Peter 2:24 (NLT) " He personally carried our sins in his body on the cross so that we can be dead to sin and live for what is right. By His wounds you are healed"

He personally carried each one of our individual sins upon the cross. He knew you. He knows you. And, He died for you!

"THE CROSS IS OUR FREEDOM!"

_____

_____

_____

_____

_____

_____

_____

_____

_____

_____

_____

_____

31

We think food is the real nourishment we need for our bodies. How much greater is God's Word REAL NOURISHMENT to our souls! You feel the difference it makes, RIGHT NOW, when you eat of it! It even effects the mind and body!

_____

_____

_____

_____

_____

_____

_____

_____

_____

_____

_____

_____

_____

_____

_____

_____

32

Luke 18:42 (NIV)

Jesus said to him, "Receive your sight; your faith has healed you." 43 Immediately he received his sight and followed Jesus, praising God. When all the people saw it, they also praised God.

The Lord is faithful to take the world out of us. We can sometimes look upon following the Lord as a dry desert with no pleasure, but rather only admonishment and punishment for our sins, or a land of 'no's to our cravings. But, His Word shows different. It is a land of 'Yes's. He asks the blind man, "Do you want to see?" The blind man answers, "Yes Lord, heal my eyes!" And Jesus heals and opens the eyes of the blind man. Can we actually visualize in our minds what that would be like to all of a sudden be able to see? We would be doing some out of this world dancing and ready to follow this man anywhere. Where are we today? Are we still hooked on this worlds pleasures that lead us only to be chained as slaves and eventually be destroyed by the very things that are our pleasure? Is this our land of escape and pleasure we choose to live in? Is it leading us to abundant life? The Lord Jesus is actually not offering us a dry barren land of 'no's, but He is offering us actual real abundant life. Jesus, open our eyes so that we, who say we can see, but can really be the blind ones, will have our eyes opened by You so that we can really see all the freedom and ecstatic joy You are calling us to and run for it. We are called by the Lord to be powerful in this life and to walk on higher plains of freedom from this world. Peace

---

33

WE ARE CALLED TO WALK THROUGH THE FIRE UNBURNT! Why? Because we are NOT of this world.

1 Peter 2:11 (NLT) "Dear friends, I warn you as "temporary residents and foreigners" to keep away from worldly desires that wage war against your very souls."

So, the sins I may easily slip into are actually waging war against me. They are not there for my benefit, as they promote themselves to be. No, they are there to kill me. My soul needs to be free to hear from God, to praise Him, and be able to, with freedom, love other people. Jesus freed us from the chains to this world. We just 'fly away'. But for now, we remain in this world, not to be chained, enslaved, by it, but to be powerful influencers for His kingdom in the midst.

_____

_____

_____

_____

_____

_____

_____

_____

_____

_____

_____

34

Some days we may feel like we just need some HELP. For those who have TURNED to their SHEPHERD, there is good news.

1 Peter 2:25 (NLT) "Once you were like sheep who wandered away. But now you have turned to your Shepherd, the GUARDIAN OF YOUR SOULS."

Looking up the definition of 'guardian' I found, "One who looks after, protects, or defends." We've got God all around us today. He's got this! Thanks to our loving heavenly Father who loves and takes care of our souls today.

_____

_____

_____

_____

_____

_____

_____

_____

_____

_____

_____

_____

_____

35

A WORD for strength today. Let us be reminded to SPEAK.

"If you speak good words rather than worthless ones, you will be my spokesman. You must influence them; do not let them influence you!"

Jeremiah 15:19 (NLT)

_____

_____

_____

_____

_____

_____

_____

_____

_____

_____

_____

_____

_____

_____

_____

_____

Words & title of Rich Mullins song. READY FOR THE STORM. I would ask please that you listen to it today. https://m.youtube.com/watch?v=B9wP0xAg02E The Spirit will bless you.

Hebrews 10:34-38 (NLT) " you suffered along with those who were thrown into jail, and when all you owned was taken from you, you accepted it with joy. You knew there were better things waiting for you that will last forever. So, do not throw away this confident trust in the Lord. Remember the great reward it brings you! Patient endurance is what you need now, so that you will continue to do God's will. Then you will receive all that he has promised. 'For in just a little while, the Coming One will come and not delay. And my righteous ones will live by faith but I will take no pleasure in anyone who turns away.' But we are not like those who turn away from God to their own destruction. We are the faithful ones, whose Souls will be saved."

The spiritual, transformational place of pure victory we are called to live in.

REVELATION 12:11,12 "And they have defeated him by the BLOOD of the LAMB and by their TESTIMONY. And they did NOT LOVE their lives so much that they were AFRAID TO DIE.

Therefore, rejoice, O heavens! And YOU will live in the heavens, REJOICE!"

38

Fellow brothers and sisters, we have a job! It is greater than any, although they can be good, worldly job. Our heavenly job today is to TRUST IN GOD.

Isaiah 49:23 (NLT)

"...Those who trust in me shall NEVER be put to shame."

_____

_____

_____

_____

_____

_____

_____

_____

_____

_____

_____

_____

_____

_____

39

Proverbs 19:11 (NIV) "A person's wisdom yields PATIENCE; it is to one's glory to OVERLOOK an offense."

Both refer to FREEDOM. Wisdom, and following it, quell the internal storms, and give patience, because we lean upon our all-powerful, loving Fathers will to be done upon earth as it is in heaven. Overlooking an offense frees us from holding on to vengeance which can ultimately destroy us. Overlooking an offense only makes us stronger. Again, because we are trusting in God to take care of us, not man's opinions or actions. In an evil world of tyranny and corruption God wants His children to remain FREE.

_____

_____

_____

_____

_____

_____

_____

_____

_____

_____

_____

_____

_____

40

My child you can get so caught up in the perceived injustices of this world, and you are not wrong, because I have made you to be able to see them. But, I am calling you up now, to see, and fight the higher realms of battle. 2 Cor 10:3,4 (NLT) "We are human, but we don't wage war as humans do. We use God's mighty weapons, not worldly weapons, to knock down the strongholds of human reasoning and to destroy false arguments.

_____

_____

_____

_____

_____

_____

_____

_____

_____

_____

_____

_____

_____

_____

41

What is one thing that defeats the enemy's attacks in our lives today? Being JOYFUL. Yes, believe it or not, it is a CHOICE we have to make. His will for our lives, His promises for our lives, do not change based upon the trials we face. Being joyful is a statement we make that puts out the devil's flames.

1 Thessalonians 5:16-18 (NLT)

"Always be joyful. Never stop praying. Be thankful in all circumstances, for this is God's will for you who belong to Christ Jesus."

_____

_____

_____

_____

_____

_____

_____

_____

_____

_____

_____

_____

_____

42

When I feel a lack of strength, or distant from God, if I go to God's WORD I can be TRANSFORMED in a flash!

Psalm 119:28 (NIV)

"My soul is weary with sorrow; strengthen me according to your word.

_____

_____

_____

_____

_____

_____

_____

_____

_____

_____

_____

_____

_____

_____

_____

43

Yea though I walk through the valley of the shadow of death, no evil shall I fear. Why? Because, YOUR KINGDOM, Almighty God, is with me! Your rod, your staff, are always by my side. In You I shall be healed....

Mark 12:33,34 (NLT)

"And I know it is important to love Him with all my heart and all my understanding and all my strength, and to love my neighbor as myself. This is more important than to offer all of the burnt offerings and sacrifices required in the law." Realizing how much the man understood, Jesus said to him, "You are NOT FAR from the KINGDOM of God."

So, let us try to really LOVE God today, and let the love, that only the Holy Spirit can give us (this is the next step that puts us from being 'NOT FAR, but rather, INTO the kingdom of God) help us to reach out to our neighbors and 'love them as we love ourselves.' This may take a conscious effort, but this order can only be fulfilled by the Holy Spirit now dwelling within. Let us be filled up with His power today.

_____

_____

_____

_____

_____

_____

_____

_____

_____

44

I love the words Jesus spoke to the man that had said, 'It is better to love the Lord your God with your whole heart, and to love your neighbor as yourself, than to offer all the burnt sacrifices.'. Jesus said he was not far from the KINGDOM OF GOD. That sounds pretty good. Well, truth is, instead of being 'not far' wouldn't we rather be 'IN' the KINGDOM OF GOD? In the Super Bowl would you rather be, at the end, 'not far' from winning, or, actually winning. Who holds up the trophy? I believe Jesus shows us the way to be, not on the edge, but IN.

Romans 14:17 (NLT)

"For the KINGDOM OF GOD is not a matter of what we eat or drink but of living a life of goodness and peace and joy in the HOLY SPIRIT." Yeah, there's that Holy Spirit again! Yeah, the ONE Jesus promised to send us! The One we need to enter the KINGDOM OF GOD with! The Holy Spirit is poured out on us by the ONE who says, "Come!". Being a good, and wise, person gets us close, but the Holy Spirit is our ticket to ENTER and PARTAKE. Being a good person and following a Christian religion is a good thing, but it only leads us to a door. A door we must enter, partake, and be TRANSFORMED!

_____

_____

_____

_____

_____

_____

_____

_____

45

If there be, in our own personal worlds, today, any worries or anxieties that beset us. Let us know this, GOD has already personally won the VICTORY for us over that specific, maybe tormenting, situation. Since HE has already achieved the victory over that which comes against us, let us CHOOSE to grab ahold of HIS victory and not the enemies lie. Let's reside in HIS camp today!

PHILIPPIANS 4:6,7 (NLT)

"Don't worry about anything; instead, pray about everything. Tell God what you need, and thank him for all he has done. Then you will experience GOD'S PEACE, which exceeds anything we can understand. His peace will guard your hearts and Minds as you live in Christ Jesus."

_____

_____

_____

_____

_____

_____

_____

_____

_____

_____

_____

_____

46

Wouldn't we love to be able to say that we are actually mature and complete, not lacking anything. Sounds a bit arrogant. BUT, when God does the work in us we can just RECEIVE it and REST in it. No more worries, no more frustrations, no more striving. We are good. Maybe we won't experience being complete, completely, until the gate of heaven is opened for us. However, maybe there is another heavenly dimension that we can experience now. Maybe we have just had the so called, "Wool been pulled over our eyes.", to believe we cannot go there. We can live in and be transformed by GOD'S KINGDOM NOW, in this world. However, we must follow JESUS and His WORD. He will take us on this journey to the places we must go.

JAMES 1:2-4 (NIV)

"Consider it pure joy, my brothers and sisters, whenever you face trials of many kinds, because you know that the testing of your faith produces PERSEVERANCE. Let perseverance finish its work so that you may BE MATURE and COMPLETE, not LACKING ANYTHING."

The Lord's Word also touches our daily functioning in RELATIONSHIPS. Our transformation by the Holy Spirit not only changes our spiritual identity. Yes, it does, but it changes our relationships with others as well. We must LISTEN and ACT.

Philippians 4:2 (NLT) "...Please, because you BELONG to the Lord, SETTLE your disagreement."

_____

_____

_____

_____

_____

_____

_____

_____

_____

_____

_____

_____

_____

48

Isaiah 40:31 (NIV) "but those who hope in the LORD will renew their strength. They will soar on wings like eagles; they will run and not grow weary, they will walk and not be faint." Psalm 23:3 (NKJV) "HE RESTORES MY SOUL."

Yes, Lord, I need this strength today. However, who or from what source am I relying on to receive it from? The Almighty, the Lifter of my head, the Beginning and the End, let us yield and surrender to Him today. The One True God. The lover of our souls!

_____

_____

_____

_____

_____

_____

_____

_____

_____

_____

_____

49

FASTING in the bible! Mentioned over 70 times. A discipline used throughout the Old and New Testaments, and throughout church history.

Joel 2:12,13 (NLT) "That is why the Lord says, 'Turn to me now, while there is time. Give Me your HEARTS. Come with FASTING, weeping, and mourning. Don't tear your clothing in your grief, but tear your HEARTS instead.'"

Do we want, and seek after, high spiritual experiences? Sometimes we can seek after the highs, the spiritual gifts, which we definitely should seek and ask for, while leaving the horse behind the cart. In seeking these gifts, there can be a step missing, and that is God wants our hearts given to Him. He does not just want an outward display of power and repentance. He wants us to repent inwardly. Tear your HEARTS. "God's desire is not to punish, but to forgive and restore His people."

_____

_____

_____

_____

_____

_____

_____

_____

_____

_____

_____

James 1:27 (NIV)

"Religion that God our Father accepts as pure and faultless is this: to look after orphans and widows in their distress and to keep oneself from being POLLUTED by the WORLD."

To be able to bring help to those who are truly in need is the richness of life. Not being POLLUTED by the world comes from sitting at Jesus feet and listening to and receiving His teaching. Here is another scripture, we all know, that are Jesus very words to us about coming to Him, listening to Him, and receiving from Him so that we may find true rest for our souls, the opposite effect of being POLLUTED by this world. Matthew 11 "Then Jesus said, come to me, all of you who are weary and carry heavy burdens, and I will give you rest. Take my yoke upon you. LET ME TEACH YOU, because I am humble and gentle at heart, and you will find rest for your souls. For my yoke is easy to bear, and the burden I give you is light. "

We are TRULY RICH if we have these two things from the book of James scripture above, and greater than any worldly wealth is "rest for your souls."

_____

_____

_____

_____

_____

_____

_____

_____

51

Reading Revelations this morning. You know, everything IS GOOD with God. He is still on the throne. All is well. We have our worries and stresses down here, but all is GOOD WITH GOD, and He promises that all will, is, and will be well with us as well. We can, and should, enter into His throne room with thanksgiving. Why? Because He promises to be with us and bring us HOME SAFELY. He will clear the way. I felt I heard him say also that its okay to bring some LAUGHTER in as well. In the midst of the trials, good times or difficult, God can give us laughter and it pierces the plans of the enemy. God is good, and you are His business.

_____

_____

_____

_____

_____

_____

_____

_____

_____

_____

_____

_____

_____

_____

52

I AM TELLING YOU THERE IS A MOVE OF GOD COMING, BUT IT IS NOT COMING THROUGH THE POPULAR MEGA CHURCH PREACHERS, TEACHERS, PASTORS, AND TELEVANGELISTS. NO, IT IS COMING THROUGH YOU! YOU WHO THINK YOUR GIFTS MAY BE SMALL AND ARE AFRAID TO USE THEM. IT IS COMING THROUGH THE SEEMINGLY COMMON PEOPLE WHO WILL NOW STAND, USE THEIR GIFTS AND SPEAK. DONT THINK YOUR GIFTS ARE TOO SMALL. EVERYTHING GIVEN BY GOD IS HUGE!

Acts 2:17 (NLT)"I WILL POUR OUT MY SPIRIT ON ALL PEOPLE...." Because of God's great love for His children, He knows how weak we are, He has made it rather easy to be saved. Why is it easy? It is easy, for us, because of the great price HE PAID to save us! God has appointed Jesus to be the judge of the living and the dead. And, His Word says that ALL who call upon the name of the Lord shall be saved! If you believe In YOUR HEART that Jesus died and was risen from the dead for you, you have eternal life. Because He loves us so much, even if we were on our death bed, were full of sin and shame, and could never do another good act for anyone, if we just call upon His name, from our heart, we are saved. This is why He died. For YOU and me. None of us, no matter how good we are, could ever EARN heaven by our actions. It is by His work, on the cross, that WE ARE SAVED! Please! If you have not already, receive what He did for us and call upon His NAME today!

_____

_____

_____

_____

_____

_____

53

Where else would we want to LOOK FOR LIFE today? He is the LIGHT to every nation, to Israel, the U.S., Russia, India, Iran and Afghanistan. He is the light to the WHOLE WORLD, every nation. When we can sit and LISTEN and speak with Him, the actual LIGHT of LIFE ITSELF, where else would we want to be?! When we experience JESUS, we lose affinity to this world.

John 8:12 (NIV)

"When JESUS spoke again to the people, he said, "I am the light of the world. Whoever follows me will never walk in darkness, but will have the light of life."

_____
_____
_____
_____
_____
_____
_____
_____
_____
_____
_____
_____
_____

For revival It does not matter how much you know. What matters is who is with you and who you know. "They will call him Emmanuel. Which means 'God is with us.' " Matt 1:23 (NLT). Is God with you?

_____

_____

_____

_____

_____

_____

_____

_____

_____

_____

_____

_____

_____

_____

_____

_____

GOOD DEEDS! Jesus undid the works of the devil, freeing us from sin and its awful consequences, so that we can have relationship with Him, AND, DO GOOD DEEDS! NLT study notes 1 John 2:28,29 (Life Application Study Bible), "Good deeds cannot produce salvation, but they are necessary proof that true faith is actually present." He freed us then to love one another and to do GOOD DEEDS to our Christian family when there is a need. Are we a bit burdened and bored with life? Good news! He has freed us today to go and do some GOOD DEEDS! WHAT can we do today? Whose life can we touch with God's love?

_____

_____

_____

_____

_____

_____

_____

_____

_____

_____

_____

_____

_____

_____

56

Our work is to BREAK the work of the enemy in our own and other's lives. So, whatever we have NEGATIVE that we do, or negative thoughts about ourselves that we may have are gone right NOW! Our REAL identity is not an insecure negative identity. There is nothing about ourselves that we can't like. We are perfect in Christ. Our TRUE IDENTITY is hidden in Christ and we are ok. No need to worry about anything. Anything that comes to our minds that puts us down, or oppresses us, just rebuke them in Jesus name! Don't let those demons hang around. Yes, we are in a war, and not of the flesh! Let's keep our heads held high. Even if we have stumbled. His grace and kindness still covers us. Trust in what He did, and not what we ourselves have done, and get up! Let Him lift our heads and take us to HIGHER PLACES.

Psalm 62:1,2 (NLT) "I wait quietly before God, for my victory comes from him. He alone is my rock and my salvation, my fortress where I will never be shaken."

Our THOUGHTS and GOD'S thoughts. Scripture teaches us that God's thoughts are way above ours. Yet, the Bible also says we can have the mind of Christ. So, God can give us new thoughts not merely generated from our own human mind, but divinely given to us by His Holy Spirit within us. BUT, WE MUST GO THERE. We must be willing to ALLOW Him to change the way we think. Sometimes, we may not allow Him in because we really dont want to change our ways of thinking. We don't want to come up higher. But, He remains there, ready to EMPOWER us today. If, we let Him.

1 John 2:27 (NLT) "But you have received the Holy spirit, and he lives Within you, so you don't need anyone to teach you what is true. For the spirit teaches you everything you need to know. And what he teaches is true--it is not a lie. So just as he taught you, remain in fellowship with Christ."

_____

_____

_____

_____

_____

_____

_____

_____

_____

_____

The enemy is always trying to get our eyes off this fact. This scriptural fact below is the truth Every day. TODAY. This is true TODAY! We can worship Him in this realm today. The enemy wants us to get our eyes off of Him, and get our eyes on the worries of tomorrow or the happenings of yesterday. We can worship him TODAY and walk in His kingdom glory, where we walk through the flames, we toss off the snakes, we walk on water, and we are filled with joy. Because, we are not of this world. Worship Him TODAY!

Isaiah 6:3 (NIV)

"And they were calling to one another: "Holy, holy, holy is the LORD Almighty; the whole earth is full of his glory.""

_____

_____

_____

_____

_____

_____

_____

_____

_____

_____

_____

Zechariah 2:13 (NIV)

"BE STILL before the LORD, all mankind, because he has ROUSED Himself from His holy dwelling."

When the LORD is going to act it's not up to, or about us, being busy with actions, or how we may pray. It's about being still, on our knees, and WORSHIPING HIM who is the Ruler of all. God is Almighty!

_____

_____

_____

_____

_____

_____

_____

_____

_____

_____

_____

_____

_____

Colossians 1:22 (NLT)

What is our standing before God TODAY? Is He judging us for our many errors? Do we need to do better before we can regain His presence with us, or His love? Remember, the devil is a liar. Here is our TRUE position:

"Yet now he has reconciled you to himself through the death of Christ in his physical body. As a result, he has brought you into his own presence, and YOU ARE HOLY and blameless as you stand before him WITHOUT a SINGLE FAULT."

Have a guilt free day everyone! Be free! Our heavenly Father LOVES us, APPROVES of us, and is WITH us! ENJOY LIFE! What wonderful LOVE He has for His children. All we have to do is receive it and WE ARE CHANGED!

61

A scripture that is mind-blowing!!! We are the privileged children of God.

"So, don't boast about following a particular human leader. For everything belongs to you, whether Paul or Apollo's or Peter, or the world, or life and death, or the present and the future. Everything belongs to you, and you belong to Christ, and Christ belongs to God."

1 Corinthians 3:21-23. (NLT)

One of my songs 'Created to Be Free' has a lyric in it, "Don't need no ticket 'cause I own this place

And if you falter I will show you grace

Created to be free

62

However we may do this, EXALT JESUS! WELCOME TO THE WORLD OF BEING FORGIVEN FOR ETERNITY!!!

From NLT Study Guide LUKE 22:

"Jesus instituted a NEW COVENANT (agreement) between God and his people. Under this new covenant, Jesus would die in the place of sinners. Unlike the blood of animals, his blood (because he is God) would remove the sins of all who put their faith in him. Jesus SACRIFICE would never have to be repeated; it would be good for all eternity. Prophets looked forward to this NEW covenant that would fulfill the Old sacrificial agreement, and John the Baptist called Jesus, "The Lamb of God who TAKES AWAY the SIN of the WORLD." This, of course, includes OUR individual sins. Wait! Please don't let this go. The devil, our minds are a battle field, may try to take away the importance of this in our daily lives. Know Jesus! He is our savior for eternity! The New Covenant. John the Baptist said, "I baptize with water, but the One coming, will baptize with FIRE!" If we want some of that 'fire', HE said He would give it. Who are we to say, "Nope, that's not for me."

_____

_____

_____

_____

_____

_____

_____

_____

63

For WHAT do you SEEK? Sounds like a line out of Monty Python and the Holy Grail. Within the church (the body of Christ), what do we seek? Do we seek for status and power?

Luke 22:27 (NLT) "Who is more important, the one who sits at the table or the one who serves? The one who sits at the table, of course. But not here! For I am among you as one who serves." Jesus words. Living in the kingdom of God is a PARADOX. Like we must die to ourselves to truly live. In the NLT study notes it says, " Jesus defined true leadership as service--meeting the needs of others and empowering them to be all that God has called them to be. This statement was striking in a culture for which status and power were Central."

WHAT DO YOU SEEK? True service comes from a heart of loving others by seeing them as God wants us to see them, and investing action in their lives. God's Spirit changes our answer to "WHAT DO YOU SEEK?"

64

I love Jesus' WORDS.

We should not compare our worth, position, or what God has personally called US TO DO with others. Our identity comes, truly, from Jesus alone.

John 21:22 (NLT) "Jesus replied, "If I want him to remain alive until I return, what is that to you? AS FOR YOU, follow me." We are not to compare ourselves to others. We are so uniquely created and gifted for His purpose for our lives. SHINE!

_____

_____

_____

_____

_____

_____

_____

_____

_____

_____

_____

_____

_____

Our enemy, Satan, deceitfully tries to work his way into our lives, and minds, to take away our LOVE FOR OTHERS. God's word says, 'Those who are forgiven much, love much'. We are FREE because we ARE FORGIVEN, and because we are forgiven we LOVE others. Faith, is what saves us, and faith expresses itself through love of God and others. So, we can use our LOVE OF OTHERS as a monitor of faith. Is our love of others being crushed? Do we feel judgement, criticalness, offense, bitterness, resentment, sneaking into our relationships, choking out the flow of God's love? This is one thing our enemy slyly and covertly does to extinguish our God connected flames. I was on a walk around the neighborhood the other day and I was having a difficult time, mentally and emotionally, getting my mind off an egregious situation that had occurred a while back by a person in the neighborhood. As I was walking, stewing in the mental frustration, I walked by a young child and his mother who were working in their front yard. The young child called out, 'Hi!', 'Hi', I responded. He added, 'how are you doing?' 'Good!', I said, "How are you?" He responded with a "Good.", and he added after a hesitation, "Nice to meet you!" (I think his mom was training him). Amazing! The devil was insidiously trying to bring division against others, and division within myself, in effect, turning off the flow of love and caring to others, and then it was profoundly reeled back in by a child. This is what it is about. The channel of love, and caring for, and kindness, towards others seen in an act by a child brought me back to truth. I am here, not for vengeance, or to become, by offense, distant from others. But rather, I found the SWEETNESS of engaging in, and caring for others in the action of a child.

Truly I tell you," He said, Matthew 18:3 (NIV) "Unless you change and become like little children, you will never enter the kingdom of heaven."

_____

_____

_____

_____

Wouldn't it be great if today's news headlines read:

NO WORRIES NEEDED TODAY!

Matthew 6:26,27 (NIV)

26 "Look at the birds of the air; they do not sow or reap or store away in barns, and yet your heavenly Father feeds them. Are you not much more valuable than they? 27 Can any one of you by worrying add a single hour to your life?"

How much faith is enough? Do good things only happen in and through our lives because we created them through FAITH? No, God is the Ultimate Creator and He has a plan for our lives in HIS Kingdom. His WILL - WILL be done, on earth as it is in heaven. When we pray, we ENLIVEN God's WILL, not ours. It's not our super strong FAITH that gets whatever we are praying for done, it's His WILL. The fact that we prayed at all shows FAITH. And remember, Jesus said all it takes to move a mountain is faith the size of a mustard seed. If it was GOD'S WILL, not just ours, to move that mountain, the mountain will move when you pray. If it is not God's will, we can have the greatest faith of all time, and say what we think are the right formula of words in our prayer, and that mountain WILL NOT move. We do not LEAD God. God LEADS us. So, todays WORRIES be gone. God has the perfect GOOD WILL for our lives today. So, let's listen to our Abba Father today and pray that His kingdom come AND His WILL be done today 'ON EARTH AS IT IS IN HEAVEN.' And know this, that God's divine shield will surround us today. God wants the father/child intimate relationship with us. We come before Him and ASK and His GOOD divine will, WILL BE DONE (not always our own will)! When we are in this RELATIONSHIP we have no need to WORRY. Ask and trust.

_____

_____

_____

Let us not forget, JESUS IS GOD. When we pray, please remember, that there is POWER and AUTHORITY in HIS NAME. He does hear when we pray and His LOVE is ALWAYS with us. One of the exciting things of prayer is not that what we ask for may or may not happen, because it happens according to His perfect will, not ours. But, we can be, and are, always CHANGED.

WHO is JESUS?

Colossians 1:15-20 (NLT)

"Christ is the visible image of the invisible God. He existed before anything was created and is SUPREME over all creation, for through HIM God created everything in the HEAVENLY REALMS and on EARTH. He made the things we can see and the things we can't see such as thrones, kingdoms, rulers, and authorities in the UNSEEN WORLD. Everything was created through HIM and FOR HIM. He existed before anything else and he holds all creation together. Christ is also the head of the church which is his body. He is the beginning, Supreme Over All Who rise from the dead. So, he is first in everything. For God in all his fullness was pleased to live in Christ, and through him God reconciled everything to himself. He made peace with everything in heaven and on Earth by means of Christ's Blood on the cross."

_____

_____

_____

_____

_____

_____

_____

Let us not waste our life on "SMOKE". Smoke screens that arise in our lives that take us away from pursuing the ONE THING that truly matters and can FULFILL us. Instead, we may carry worries and anxieties about things that have, or may, happen in this world. Or, I may focus on a condition of mine, like being overweight, for example. Like correcting this, or trying to control any condition, will bring me fulfillment or peace with myself. SMOKE SCREEN! Instead of me CONTROLLING and OBSESSING with anything, I should raise my arm up to the sky and allow the Lord to take it and allow Him to literally lift me to HIGHER PLACES. When I am in His higher places I can see more clearly and be FREED from that which calls me and consumes me from this world. We are IN this world, but not OF it. We look for answers WITHIN this world to deal with matters besetting us. But, if we seek and allow Him to be our answer, we are freed. TRUSTING in, RELYING on, and RECEIVING His actual presence in the Holy Spirit, will give us NEW perspectives that will truly FREE us, mind, body and spirit. GO HIGHER!

Colossians 2:6,7 (NLT) "And now, just as you accepted Christ JESUS as your LORD, you must continue to FOLLOW HIM. Let your ROOTS grow down INTO HIM, and let your LIVES be BUILT on him. Then your faith will GROW STRONG in the truth you were taught and you will OVERFLOW with THANKFULLNESS."

_____

_____

_____

_____

_____

_____

69

The 11TH Commandment! What?

We all know the 10 Commandments. You could call this one the 11TH COMMANDMENT. John 13:34,35 (NLT) "so now I am giving you a NEW commandment: Love each other. Just as I have loved you, you should love each other. Your love for one another will prove to the world that you are my disciples."

Loving others is not a new commandment. But, loving others AS JESUS loved them IS. Jesus loved people as God loved people. We now, must love people as Jesus loved. It is by this revolutionary, SACRIFICIAL love that we will bring others to Christ and help unite the church. It is hard to imagine actually loving others as Jesus, God Himself, loves others, but this is our deeper calling. So, Jesus, we pray. Let our love for others be radical today! Your Word says we can have the mind of Christ. So, CHANGE US so that we may receive and allow the HOLY SPIRIT to change even the way we think of others today. So that, we may love them not with just our own love, but actually with the love of Jesus. Amen. To love others AS JESUS DID, is not a suggestion. It is a COMMANDMENT! Let us think on this. We CAN do it! AND, as we do this we will also be freed from any chains that may bind us in this world.

_____

_____

_____

_____

_____

_____

_____

70

BEING CHRISTIANS- AND REALIZING THAT 'WE ARE NOT OF THIS WORLD', WHY DO WE CONTINUE TO SEEK OUR NEEDS AND DESIRES FROM IT?

Psalm 127:1 (NIV)

_____

_____

_____

_____

_____

_____

_____

_____

_____

_____

_____

_____

_____

_____

_____

"Unless the LORD builds the house, the builders labor in vain. Unless the LORD watches over the city, the guards stand watch in vain."

When we pray, and rely upon the move of God He moves into our situations and changes them for our and others good with divine action. Things become exciting when we see God moving in our lives. So, Lord Jesus, we ask, that whatever seemingly unsurmountable walls that may confront us today be taken down and Lord Jesus we ask that you work within these situations and bring Your miraculous changes so that Your will be done in these situations ON EARTH AS IT IS IN HEAVEN. Amen and

PEACE.

_____

_____

_____

_____

_____

_____

_____

_____

_____

_____

_____

72

Someone posted this saying below on Facebook. Brilliant: "Some say life is short so you better enjoy it, but ETERNITY is LONG so you better PREPARE for it."

Below are the words of Peter in Acts 2:36-40 (NLT), but it's as if they are words being spoken to us in our generation RIGHT NOW.

"'So, let everyone in Israel know for certain that God has made this JESUS, whom you crucified, to be both Lord and Messiah!' Peter's words pierced their hearts, and they said to him and to the other apostles, 'Brothers what should we do?' Peter replied, 'Each of you must REPENT of YOUR SINS and turn to God and be BAPTIZED in the name of Jesus Christ for the FORGIVENESS of your SINS. THEN you will RECEIVE the gift of the HOLY SPIRIT. This PROMISE is to you, and to your children, and even to the Gentiles--all who have been CALLED by the Lord our God.' Then Peter continued preaching FOR A LONG TIME, strongly urging all his listeners, 'Save yourselves from this CROOKED GENERATION!'"

Let him who has ears to hear....

_____

_____

_____

_____

_____

_____

_____

_____

73

TRY IT! Take some God given authority and command! Not for anything and everything of course. But, He did give us His authority to heal all kinds of sickness and to cast out demons. There is a time to be bold and speak. Exercise some God given POWER. Don't worry about not being humble. Being humble is to do things God's way and not our own. Being humble is relying on God's power and not our own. If He gave authority to us to use, then use it! The power to change things for His purpose.

Acts 16:18 (NLT)

"This went on day after day until Paul got so exasperated that he turned and said to the demon within her, ' I COMMAND you in the name of Jesus Christ to come out of her. ' And instantly it left her."

Are there anything in our lives that need to be commanded to? Try it.

_____

_____

_____

_____

_____

_____

_____

_____

_____

_____

Please don't let the day slip by without prayer and thankfulness. POWER and AUTHORITY! It will change things and make the critical difference in our lives today.

Luke 10:17 (NLT)

"When the 72 disciples returned, they JOYFULLY reported to him, "Lord, even the demons obey us when we use your name!" "Yes," He told them, I saw Satan fall from heaven like lightning! LOOK, I have given you authority OVER ALL THE POWER of the ENEMY, and you can walk among snakes and scorpions and Crush them. Nothing will injure you. But DON'T REJOICE because evil spirits obey you; REJOICE because your names are REGISTERED IN HEAVEN."

_____
_____
_____
_____
_____
_____
_____
_____
_____
_____
_____
_____

God vast. Beyond our knowledge. But, we can, if we choose to, know Him, as He reveals Himself to us in our daily journeys, walks of life.

Acts 10:19,20 (NLT)

"meanwhile, as Peter was puzzling over the vision, the Holy Spirit said to him, "Three men have come looking for you. Get up, go downstairs, and go with them without hesitation. Don't worry for I have sent them."

Yes, what an amazing journey of life we can be on if we allow the All Powerful, Infinite God to rule and speak into our lives. Get ready to have our minds expanded as the Holy Spirit speaks into our lives. He is daily with us creating and leading our journey. Give us the gift of Your Holy Spirit and help us to hear from you today Daddy Abba Father. Amen

_____

_____

_____

_____

_____

_____

_____

_____

_____

_____

_____

_____

TRIALS are stepping stones to LETTING GO.

MATTHEW 16:23-25 (BSB)

""You are a stumbling block to Me. For you do not have in mind the things of God, but the things of men." 24 Then Jesus told His disciples, "If anyone wants to come after Me, he must DENY HIMSELF and take up his cross and follow Me. 25 For whoever wants to save his life will lose it, but whoever loses his life for My sake will find it...."

When life's trials present themselves (daily it may seem) we have the OPPORTUNITY to face them with our own thoughts and emotions, we can act on them with our human understanding,

or, they can be TRANSLATED by Jesus' purposes. For, how does a dead person have stress, worries and anxieties? How does a dead person get offended? HIS PURPOSE is not always our own. However, HIS PURPOSE can now be OUR PURPOSE in this life. That is to take part in Jesus' mission to SAVE others by sharing the good news with them. Jesus laid down His life for others. We should do the same. He wants to FREE OUR MINDS from that which CONSUMES us in this world so that we may be able to love and reach out to others so that they, too, might believe in Jesus.

Acts 9:42 (NLT) "The news spread through the whole town, and many BELIEVED in the Lord." May our minds be unchained today so that, regardless of what may confront us, we might think like Jesus and use it to bring others into His Kingdom.

_____

_____

_____

_____

77

Only SAY THE WORD and I WILL BE HEALED!

It's amazing. God spoke a word and this world was created. Yes, He JUST SPOKE A WORD. Jesus, being God and having ALL authority only needs to speak a word, He doesn't even have to be in their presence, and a person is healed.

Luke 7:6-10 (NLT), "So Jesus went with them. But just before they arrived at the house, the officer sent some friends to say, "Lord, don't trouble yourself by coming to my home, for I am not worthy of such an honor. I am not even worthy to come and meet you. Just SAY THE WORD from where you are and my servant will be healed. I know this because I am under the authority of my Superior officers, and I have authority over my soldiers. I only need to say, 'Go' and they go or 'Come' and they come. And if I say to my slaves 'Do this'. They do it. " when Jesus heard this, he was amazed turning to the crowd that was following him he said, "I tell you, I haven't seen Faith like this in all Israel!" and when the officers friends return to his house they found the slave completely healed." We have such an awesome God who loves us. Speak into our lives today Jesus and HEAL THE SICK! May the lost FIND YOU. STRENGTH AND HOPE TO THE WEARY. Peace.

_____

_____

_____

_____

_____

_____

_____

78

You know, the devil can't take you AWAY from Jesus, but he can sure blind you from SEEING Him. But, Jesus is always there...a STEP AWAY...we may think He is FAR... but He is NOT...His love endures forever...The disciples were in the boat in rough waters...Jesus comes walking by, on the water, and gets in the boat...the storm calms down immediately. He is always there...if we call upon Him...we will be saved. JESUS was there for the disciples then. He is here for us today.

_____

_____

_____

_____

_____

_____

_____

_____

_____

_____

_____

_____

_____

_____

You want to get to HEAVEN someday or come before the ALMIGHTY in His presence TODAY? Then, USE THE STAIRS!!!

John 1:51 (NLT) "Then He (Jesus) said, " I tell you the truth, you will all see Heaven open and the angels of God going up and down on the SON OF MAN, the one who is the STAIRWAY between HEAVEN and EARTH."

_____

_____

_____

_____

_____

_____

_____

_____

_____

_____

_____

_____

_____

_____

_____

_____

80

JESUS came to take OFF all our CHAINS, emotional, spiritual, physical. Paul had some real metal chains on him that he desired removed. Where is our, like Paul, radical Christianity, that hungered for the lost to be found, even leading to real metal chains? It is there inside of us! Let the Lord light the fire!

Jesus, we ask You remove ALL CHAINS, real metal, and all emotional, physical and spiritual chains from our lives. Also, when we align ourselves with GOD'S PURPOSE for our lives, to know Him and to make Him known, our chains are released and we are FREE.

Jesus give us the FIRE of the Holy Spirit to seek out Your children who are lost!

Early Acts days Christianity when they all shared their wealth with the community. Did that equal socialism? Did that equal everyone's right to be given an income and/or be fed? No! Read the whole story.

2 Thessalonians 3:6-10 (NLT)

"And now, dear brothers and sisters, we give you this COMMAND in the name of our Lord Jesus Christ: STAY AWAY from all believers who LIVE IDLE LIVES and don't follow the tradition they received from us. For you know that you ought to IMITATE us. We were NOT IDLE when we were with you. We never accepted food from anyone without paying for it. We work hard day and night so we would not be a burden to any of you. We certainly had the right to ask you to feed us, but we wanted to give you an example to follow. Even while we were with you, we gave you this command: "Those UNWILLING to WORK will NOT get to EAT." Doesn't this go against a 'woke' society that thinks they have a right to be taken care of by the giving of others blood, sweat and tears?

_____

_____

_____

_____

_____

_____

_____

_____

_____

_____

82

When you need saving there is nothing greater than to be saved. Many years ago, I was riding in a Guatemalan bus packed with people. We were heading down a steep winding mountain road with sheer cliff drop offs of hundreds or more feet. Suddenly, the braking system broke with a loud snap and we were free flying down the winding road. As the bus was picking up speed and the driver was trying, without the desired effect, to slam us to a stop against the cliff walls, people began to scream. They were screaming what seemed to be their inevitable final 'death' screams, as we were destined to go over one of the many ledges of the winding curves. Some jumped off the bus as it was plowing faster and faster to its destined launch off a ledge. I heard later that some who jumped off were killed. I got down on the bus floor and anchored myself with my arms to the seat's railings, preparing for the coming impact. In total need of saving I screamed out, "Jesus stop this bus!" It immediately slammed against a small area of rock on the side of the ledge and stopped! This happened right as we were about to arrive at a curve in the road that was actually named, "La Curva De La Muerte" or, "The Curve of Death". In fear of it may be starting to roll again, I got off that bus as quickly as I could. I walked by the front of the bus with my legs shaking. There, on the ground, was the bus driver on his knees in front of the bus with his hands raised to the heavens in thanks!

When we need being saved there is no one greater than the one who saves us!

1 Thessalonians 5:9,10 (NLT) "For God chose to SAVE us through our Lord Jesus Christ, NOT to pour out his ANGER on us. Christ died for us so that, whether we are dead or alive when he returns, we can LIVE WITH HIM FOREVER."

_____

_____

_____

_____

Words that SPEAK into our life's situations today. WORDS that go deep into our soul and speak light and 'wake up' calls to our minds.

1 Thessalonians 5:16-18 (NLT)," Always be joyful. Never stop praying. Be thankful in all circumstances, for this is God's will for you who belong to Christ Jesus. "

And here below are beautiful words from the Life Application Study Bible "Our joy, prayers, and thankfulness should not fluctuate with our circumstances or feelings. Obeying these three commands--BE JOYFUL, NEVER stop PRAYING and BE THANKFUL-- often goes against our natural inclinations. When we make a conscious decision to do what God says, however, we will begin to see people in a new perspective. When we do God's will, we will find it easier to be joyful and thankful." So, going into work today, facing any of life's blessings, or challenges, this is how we must enter the ring.

_____

_____

_____

_____

_____

_____

_____

_____

_____

_____

84

God SPEAKS to us, even today. Speak up! What God has given us we must SHARE. Be bold, be courageous! SPEAK UP!

Esther 4:14 (NIV)

"For if you remain silent at this time, relief and deliverance for the Jews will arise from another place, but you and your father's family will perish. And who knows but that you have come to your royal position for such a time as this?"

_____

_____

_____

_____

_____

_____

_____

_____

_____

_____

_____

_____

85

To move forward as Christians, becoming more like Christ, we need to get rid of the fear of what others may think of us, our worldly reputations.

Acts 11:1-3 (MSG) "The news traveled fast and in no time the leaders and Friends back in Jerusalem heard about it- heard that the non-Jewish "outsiders" were now "in". When Peter got back to Jerusalem, some of his old associates, concerned about circumcision, called him on the carpet: "What do you think you're doing rubbing shoulders with that crowd, eating what is prohibited and ruining our good name?"

Jesus, give us Your Holy Spirit that frees us from the fear of man and teaches us to live our lives concerned with what you think of us, not man.

_____

_____

_____

_____

_____

_____

_____

_____

_____

_____

_____

_____

_____

86

STRENGTH. We all need to be receiving Strength, daily, from another worldly source. God's strength includes POWER, LOVE and a SOUND MIND. This is what is offered to us daily through Jesus. It is food from another world. Yes, we will be changed!

Philippians 4:11-13 (NLT) "Not that I was ever in need, for I have learned how to be content with whatever I have. I know how to live on almost nothing or with everything. I have learned the SECRET OF LIVING in every situation, whether it is with a full stomach or empty, with plenty or little. For I CAN do everything through CHRIST who GIVES ME STRENGTH."

Jesus, we ask that you send us the Holy Spirit today, and that we may allow Him to even change the way we think today. POWER, LOVE, and a SOUND MIND.

Everybody is important to God! Everybody is called to SHINE like the SUN, in whatever place God has put us in on this earth, for Him! Do not forget all of our UNIQUE importance to Him. Do not forsake the place of influence He put each of us in to shine like the sun today!

Judges 5:31 (NIV)

"So, may all your enemies perish, LORD! But may ALL who love you be like the SUN when it rises in its strength......."

We think of the greatness and importance of all the main characters in the bible. But, what about John and Jane Doe who were living their normal lives around those great ones. YES! They were called to SHINE in their settings too! What are our individual settings today? SHINE LIKE THE SUN!

_____

_____

_____

_____

_____

_____

_____

_____

_____

_____

_____

88

1 Thessalonians 2:6 (NLT)

"As for human praise, we have never sought it from you or anyone else." When we are called by God we have to be willing to lay down what we do, or don't do, being based upon the approval of others. Embolden and empower us to hear your voice and to make it known.

_____

_____

_____

_____

_____

_____

_____

_____

_____

_____

_____

_____

_____

So, do we want to base our feelings, emotions, perceptions, actions and how we make decisions today off of the truth?

Hebrews 4:12,13 (NLT)

"For the word of God is alive and powerful. It is sharper than the sharpest two-edged sword, cutting between soul and spirit, between joint and marrow. It exposes our innermost thoughts and desires. Nothing in all creation is hidden from God. Everything is naked and exposed before His eyes, and He is the one to whom we are accountable."

_____

_____

_____

_____

_____

_____

_____

_____

_____

_____

_____

_____

_____

It is about JOY! How many of us can say we feel and have real righteousness, peace, and joy? It IS available. Maybe we may not have it because we don't pursue it or ASK for it? If we want to live in His KINGDOM NOW, we must CHOOSE, PURSUE and ASK JESUS for it. REALLY! Wouldn't we really love to have real JOY today? Romans 14:17-19 (NIV) "For the kingdom of God is not a matter of eating and drinking, but of righteousness, peace and joy in the Holy Spirit, 18 because anyone who serves Christ in this way is pleasing to God and receives human approval. Let us therefore make every effort to do what leads to peace and to mutual edification." Jesus, we ask that Your Joy affect us today.

_____

_____

_____

_____

_____

_____

_____

_____

_____

_____

_____

_____

_____

91

A warm burning fire of HOPE in the soul is given to those that TRUST God.

Romans 15:13 (NLT)

"I pray that God, the SOURCE of hope, will fill you COMPLETELY with joy and peace because you TRUST in Him. THEN you will overflow with CONFIDENT hope through the POWER of the Holy Spirit."

Peace

_____

_____

_____

_____

_____

_____

_____

_____

_____

_____

_____

_____

_____

_____

_____

Simple, but deep. God wants to strengthen us, and free us by ROOTING out our sins that we hang onto. It is so simple that we may gloss over it, or believe it is not for us, that we have higher knowledge.

2 Corinthians 12:19-21 (NLT) "Everything we do, dear friends, is to strengthen you. For I am afraid that when I come I won't like what I find, and you won't like my response. I am afraid that I will find quarreling, jealousy, anger, selfishness, slander, gossip, arrogance, and disorderly behavior. Yes, I am afraid that when I come again, God will humble me in your presence. And I will be grieved because many of you have not given up your old sins. You have not repented of your impurity, sexual immorality, and eagerness for lustful pleasure. " God's Word is always relevant and presently speaking to us. Jesus, give us your Holy Spirit that He may show us where we are to be strengthened and set free.

93

The PRESENCE OF GOD. What more is needed today? NOTHING.

2 Corinthians 12:2-4 (NLT)

"I was caught up [8]to the THIRD HEAVEN 14 years ago. Whether I was in my body or out of my body, I don't know -- only God knows. Yes, only God knows whether I was in my body or outside my body. But I do know that I was caught up to paradise and heard things so astounding that they cannot be expressed in words, things no human is allowed to tell."

The THIRD HEAVEN is a Jewish expression for the immediate presence of God. Paul wasn't sure if he was in a trance or actually taken to heaven. Though we may or may not see this awesomeness now, this is our REALITY as children of God. We can take strength today from knowing what lies ahead of us and whose presence is with us. Though we may not see it, God's PRESENCE and KINGDOM surrounds us and it is GLORIOUS!

_____

_____

_____

_____

_____

_____

_____

_____

_____

94

We have a God given purpose, GOOD DEEDS, chosen for us to do for Him this very day! Chosen for us to do before we were even born! We are a valuable gift to this world!

REV 19:7,8 (NLT)

"For the time has come for the wedding Feast of the lamb, and his bride has prepared herself. She has been given the finest of pure white linen to wear. For the fine linen represents the GOOD DEEDS of God's holy people."

In Christ, what amazing power we are in daily. Who has true authority and power in this world and the world to come? Jesus. Look what we have, THOSE WHO BELIEVE HIM, at our finger tips today.

Ephesians 1:19-23 (NLT)

"I also pray that you will understand the incredible greatness of God's power FOR US who BELIEVE Him. This is the same Mighty power that raised Christ FROM THE DEAD and seated him in the place of honor at God's right hand in the Heavenly realms. Now he is far above any ruler or authority or power or leader or anything else not only IN THIS WORLD but ALSO in the WORLD TO COME. God has put ALL THINGS under the AUTHORITY of Christ and has made him head over ALL THINGS for the benefit of the church. And the church is his body; it is made full and complete by Christ, who FILLS ALL THINGS everywhere with himself."

Power, authority and His will be done in our lives today on earth as it is in heaven.

_____

_____

_____

_____

_____

_____

_____

_____

We can run into actual and perceived problems in this life because we believe we own, or try to function in owning ourselves. We make the calls! No, we are called to be slaves.

Romans 6:19 (NLT) ".... Now you must GIVE YOURSELVES to be slaves TO RIGHTEOUS LIVING so that you will BECOME HOLY."

_____

_____

_____

_____

_____

_____

_____

_____

_____

_____

_____

_____

_____

_____

Who has control? Who has ultimate grand control? What God has said in Revelations will happen. We are not waiting to see who will win, God or Satan? To say He is not Almighty or does not have grand control, I believe, is to dethrone God. We know who wants to do this to God and exult himself.

Rev 9:14-15 (NLT) " 'Release the Four Angels who are bound at the great Euphrates River.' Then the Four Angels who had been prepared for this hour and day and month and year were turned loose to kill one third of all the people on the Earth." Below are notes from NLT Study Bible Notes on Revelation 9:15

"Hour and day and month and year: the fourfold time designation for releasing the Four Angels confirms that even evil forces must observe God's timing." God is in control and loving us today. Let us surrender to His divine will in our lives, on earth as it is in heaven. Today.

_____

_____

_____

_____

_____

_____

_____

_____

_____

_____

98

God is so good to us! He has an AMAZING PLAN for each of us. Let's let Him take the wheel. Sorry Carrie. (For using your line)

"But we are citizens of heaven, where the Lord Jesus Christ lives. And we are eagerly waiting for him to return as our Savior. He will take our weak mortal bodies and change them into glorious bodies like his own, using the same power with which he will bring EVERYTHING under HIS CONTROL. " Philippians 3:20,21 (NLT)

99

The LAST DAY is coming.

This seems to be a seldom read scripture. Words that come from God. Listen and allow the Lord to change even the way we think today.

1 Peter 1:3-5 (NLT)

"All praise to God, the Father of our Lord Jesus Christ. It is by his great Mercy that we have been BORN AGAIN, because God raised Jesus Christ from the dead. Now we live with GREAT EXPECTATION, and we have a PRICELESS INHERITANCE-an inheritance that is kept in heaven for you, pure and undefiled BEYOND the reach of change and decay. And through your faith, God is protecting you by His power until you receive this salvation, which is ready to be revealed on THE LAST DAY for all to see.

So be truly glad. There is wonderful Joy ahead, even though you have to endure many trials for a little while."

_____

_____

_____

_____

_____

_____

_____

_____

100

The Holy Spirit is a PERSON and He is God, part of the Trinity. Come speak to us and give us Your strength today. He is PERSONAL with US. Do we not want the presence, the strength of God with us today?

Acts 10:19,20 (NLT) "Meanwhile, as Peter was puzzling over the vision, the Holy Spirit SAID TO HIM, "Three men have come looking for you. Get up go downstairs, and go with them without hesitation. DON'T WORRY, for I have sent them."

We need to be reminded of WHO God is daily. Someone else's words below.

"This is significant to us as believers in Jesus today because we get to know that He is God. Whether we are encountering a difficulty or we are overcome with happiness, we are called to remember that He is God. We are invited to reflect on this truth because we have been bought at a high price."

_____

_____

_____

_____

_____

_____

_____

_____

_____

_____

_____

_____

_____

_____

_____

102

Philippians 2:6-8 (NLT)

"You must have the SAME attitude that Christ Jesus had.......he humbled himself in obedience to God and DIED a CRIMINAL'S death on a cross."

Are we sometimes too concerned about what the public may think of us if we move with Christ? Are we willing to take on societies LOWEST status as we love and SACRIFICE for others? Let's let go of the world. WE ARE CITIZENS OF HEAVEN!

_____

_____

_____

_____

_____

_____

_____

_____

_____

_____

_____

_____

_____

103

Glory to the God who made the world and everything in it. To the God who now GIVES US HIS PEACE. Yes, He is very personal with each of us.

John 14:27 (NIV)

"Peace I leave with you; my peace I give you. I do not give to you as the world gives. Do not let your hearts be troubled and do not be afraid."

What are we going through? If we are willing to receive from Him we can have PEACE IN THE MIDST.

_____

_____

_____

_____

_____

_____

_____

_____

_____

_____

_____

_____

_____

_____

BUBBLING UP!

"Jesus replied, ' anyone who drinks this water will soon become thirsty again. But those who drink the water I give will never be thirsty again. It becomes a fresh bubbling spring within them giving them eternal life.'"

......" the woman said, ' I know the Messiah is coming, the one who is called Christ. When He comes He will explain everything to us.' Then Jesus told her, 'I AM the Messiah!' " John 4:13-26 (NLT)

The Messiah! Not only was He with the woman at the well, we have the Messiah with us today! Be not afraid!

_____

_____

_____

_____

_____

_____

_____

_____

_____

_____

_____

_____

_____

105

Anxieties, worries, elections, down spiraling economies, wars, PERFECT PEACE.

2 Thessalonians 3:16 (NIV)

"Now may the Lord of peace himself give you peace at all times and in every way. The Lord be with all of you."

_____

_____

_____

_____

_____

_____

_____

_____

_____

_____

_____

_____

_____

_____

Lay it down! Let us stop trying to get God's approval, the kingdom presence, or heaven, by HUMAN EFFORT!

Galatians 4:29 & Galatians 5:1 (NLT) ".... but you are now being persecuted by those who want you to keep the law, just as Ishmael, the child born by HUMAN EFFORT, persecuted Isaac, the child born by the POWER OF THE SPIRIT........ So, Christ has truly set us free. Now make sure that you stay free, and don't get tied up again in slavery to the law." Let us ask and RECEIVE the free gift of FREEDOM by the SPIRIT now through what Christ has ALREADY DONE for us.

_____

_____

_____

_____

_____

_____

_____

_____

_____

_____

_____

_____

"So, don't boast about following a particular human leader. For everything belongs to you- whether Paul or Apollos or Peter, or the world, or life and death, or the present and the future. Everything belongs to you, and you belong to Christ, and Christ belongs to God."

1 Cor 3:21-23 (NLT)

Let us stop competing in church. We are not to see ourselves as a collection of competing interests or independent individuals. Jesus wants us UNIFIED. "Oh, we say, this or that person is a pillar of the church. And, this or that person is not yet a pillar of the church." No, we are united, and faith is the pillar.

Mercy. If God has mercy on us we should have mercy on ourselves. God is pouring out His mercy on us but we block it by believing we don't deserve it or that we need to earn it. At times, like in the election, we want certain results, so we feel we need to pray louder, pray longer, or rebuke this or that spirit, when what we really need to pray is, 'MERCY'; mercy on us as individuals, as a nation, and as a church body. The victory that we seek in all situations is found in mercy. Mercy! God's victory, Jesus going to the cross and rising from the dead, comes out of mercy. This is what we need to speak and cry out, 'Mercy'. All victory and healing of our minds, souls, and bodies is done through His Mercy. Please ask for it and receive it today. Yes, it is so glorious and it is also 'free'. He bought it for us with His life.

_____

_____

_____

_____

_____

_____

_____

_____

_____

_____

_____

_____

Mercy. It's like powerful revival. Does it come through the mighty words we may pray or does it come through mercy? It will come through His mercy.

_____

_____

_____

_____

_____

_____

_____

_____

_____

_____

_____

_____

_____

_____

_____

_____

110

My dear friends, let us not forget WHY we are still on this EARTH.

Philippians 1:27 (NLT)

"Above all, you must live as citizens of heaven, conducting yourselves in a manner worthy of the good news about Christ. Then, whether I come and see you again or only hear about you, I will know that you are standing together with ONE SPIRIT and ONE PURPOSE, FIGHTING TOGETHER for the faith, which is the GOOD NEWS. Don't be intimidated in any way by your enemies. This will be a sign to them that they are going to be destroyed, but that you are going to be saved, even by God himself. For you have been given not only the privilege of trusting in Christ but also the privilege of suffering for him. We are in this struggle together. You have seen my struggle in the past, and you know that I am still in the midst of it.

Philippians 2:1,2 (NLT) Is there any encouragement from belonging to Christ? Any comfort from his love? Any Fellowship together in the spirit? Are your hearts tender and compassionate? Then make me truly happy by agreeing wholeheartedly with each other, LOVING one another, and working TOGETHER with ONE MIND and PURPOSE."

_____

_____

_____

_____

_____

_____

_____

111

PARTNERSHIP with Jesus. Although we, ourselves, are not God, we are called to walk with the Divine One and TAKE PART in doing His divine things through His spiritual gifts.

1 Corinthians 1:4-9 (NLT)

"I always thank my God for you and for the gracious GIFTS he has given you, now that you belong to Christ Jesus. Through him, God has enriched your church in every way- with all of your eloquent words and all of your knowledge. This confirms that what I told you about Christ is true. Now you have every SPIRITUAL GIFT you need as you eagerly wait for the return of our Lord Jesus Christ. He will keep you strong to the end so that you will be free from all blame on the day when our Lord Jesus Christ returns. GOD WILL DO THIS, for he is faithful to do what he says, and he has invited you into PARTNERSHIP with his son, Jesus Christ Our Lord."

_____

_____

_____

_____

_____

_____

_____

_____

_____

_____

Special ADD:

GET WEALTHY TODAY!!!!

1 Timothy 6:6-8 (NLT)

"Yet true GODLINESS with CONTENTMENT is itself great WEALTH. After all, we brought nothing with us when we came into the world, and we can't take anything with us when we leave it. So, if we have enough food and clothing, let us be CONTENT."

_____

_____

_____

_____

_____

_____

_____

_____

_____

_____

_____

_____

_____

_____

113

Let's get READY. He's coming for His children.

Romans 2:16 (NLT)

"And this is the message I proclaim-that the day is coming when God, through Christ Jesus, will judge everyone's SECRET life."

_____

_____

_____

_____

_____

_____

_____

_____

_____

_____

_____

_____

_____

_____

_____

_____

114

Let's get ONLINE, God's net-the Bible, and get powered up. Better than coffee. Although, coffee is pretty good. God's Word-Jesus is the Word. Have a good breakfast! When God speaks to us personally, we are changed.

2 Cor 4:16 (NIV)

"Therefore, we do not lose heart. Though outwardly we are wasting away, yet inwardly we are being renewed day by day."

115

Feeling a little discouraged today about the wickedness and Evil we see flourishing in this world? Do not merely have hope in a political victory to win this battle. Take heart.

2 CHRONICLES 32:7,8 (NLT)

"Be strong and courageous! Don't be afraid or discouraged because of the king of Assyria or his mighty army, for there is a POWER FAR GREATER ON OUR SIDE! He may have a great army, but they are merely men. We have the Lord Our God to help us and to FIGHT OUR BATTLES for us!"

116

Yes, our Lord is still sovereign. New world orderers, and power hungry, satanic led politicians, you labor in vain.

Jeremiah 50:23-25 (NLT)

"Babylon the mightiest hammer in all the earth, lies broken and shattered, Babylon is desolate among the nations! Listen, Babylon, for I have set a trap for you. You are caught, for you have FOUGHT AGAINST THE LORD. The Lord has opened his Armory and brought out weapons to vent His fury against his enemies. The terror that falls upon the Babylonians will be the work of The SOVEREIGN LORD OF HEAVEN'S ARMIES." OUR KINGDOM is one of peace, love and joy. Let it not be disturbed!

117

Are we called to lead others to Christ? Yes, then we are called to be leaders. Don't get lazy and fall asleep now! Here is our TRACK. 1 Thessalonians 5:14 (NLT)

"Brothers and sisters, we urge you to WARN those who are lazy. ENCOURAGE those who are timid. Take TENDER CARE of those who are weak.

Be PATIENT with everyone.

SEE that no one pays back evil for evil, but always TRY to DO GOOD to each other and to all people. Always be JOYFUL. Never stop PRAYING. Be THANKFUL in all circumstances, for this is God's will for you who belong to Christ Jesus."

We can do it! Walk in His power!

118

WHEN WE FAIL, HIS MERCIES LIFT US. OUR WRONGS DO NOT BRING HIS CONDEMNATION. Father, thank You for Your MERCIES! We receive ALL His goodness and even miracles by His MERCIES. So, I receive Your goodness today God, because of your MERCIES. I am not left wanting because of my past mistakes.

Psalm 52:6-9 (NLT)

"The righteous will see it and be amazed. They will laugh and say, "Look what happens to Mighty Warriors who do not trust in God. They trust their wealth instead and grow more and more bold in their wickedness."

But I am like an olive tree, thriving in the house of God. I trust in God's unfailing love forever and ever. I will praise you forever, O God, for what you have done. I will wait for your MERCIES in the presence of your people."

_____

_____

_____

_____

_____

_____

_____

_____

_____

_____

119

The GREATNESS of our God. Fear Judgement for the time is near, and also, at the same time, be amazed at His astonishing creation we see around us declaring His glory. JUDGEMENT and BEAUTY, along with some amazing GRACE. I hear God saying, inviting us from His heart, to not just obey Him but to KNOW Him. He is pleading with us saying, "Know me. I am Good! Look at my creation and see I am GOOD"

Revelations 14:7 (NIV)

"He said in a loud voice, "Fear God and give Him glory, because the hour of His judgment has come. Worship him who made the heavens, the earth, the sea and the springs of water.""

_____

_____

_____

_____

_____

_____

_____

_____

_____

_____

_____

_____

_____

120

Do we ever feel like we have nothing to give. We may use the term, 'burnt out'. There is so much need, and such self, and others imposed, expectations, and feelings of our own lack of ability of what we should be doing and giving. Even while we are in the middle of feeling the lack of our own ability, Jesus says to us, "YOU FEED THEM." Then, we can marvel at His power as He seats the people in groups. He then breaks and blesses the bread and fish. He hands them out, a total of five loaves and two fish to be given to the groups making up a total of 5,000 people. With just these five loaves and two fish the people were filled up, and they even picked up 12 baskets of leftover bread and fish. When we feel we have no power, we can hear Him say, "You feed them." Philippians 4:13 (NKJV) "I can do ALL things through Christ who strengthens me." We have THE MIRACLE WORKER, the Creator of the universe, living with, and within us! We may not feel worthy or able, but He says to us, "YOU FEED THEM." We can do this today!

MARK 6:37-44 (NLT)

"By now the hour was already late. So, the disciples came to Jesus and said, "This is a desolate place, and the hour is already late. Dismiss the crowd so they can go to the surrounding countryside and villages and buy themselves something to eat."

But Jesus told them, "You give them something to eat."

They asked Him, "Should we go out and spend two hundred denarii to give all of them bread to eat?"

"Go and see how many loaves you have," He told them.

And after checking, they said, "Five—and two fish."

Then Jesus directed them to have the people sit in groups on the green grass. **40**So they sat down in groups of hundreds and fifties.

Taking the five loaves and the two fish and looking up to heaven, Jesus spoke a blessing and broke the loaves. Then He gave them to His disciples to set before the people. And He divided the two fish among them all.

They all ate and were satisfied, and the disciples picked up twelve basketfuls of broken pieces of bread and fish. And there were five thousand men who had eaten the loaves." Mark 6:35-44 (NLT)

HE is calling out to us the same today, "YOU FEED THEM."

_____

_____

_____

_____

_____

_____

122

Jesus will use whatever we have. Yes, He will take it, bless it, and multiply it. Do not fear the feeling that we may lack. Do we ever feel like we have nothing to give? We may use the term, 'burnt out'. There is so much need, and such self, and others imposed, expectations, and feelings of our own lack of ability of what we should be doing and giving. Even while we are in the middle of feeling the lack of our own ability, Jesus says to us, "YOU FEED THEM." Mark 6:37 (NLT) Then, we can marvel at His power as He seats the people in groups. He then breaks and blesses the bread and fish. He hands them out, a total of five loaves and two fish to be given to the groups making up a total of 5,000 people. With just these five loaves and two fish the people were filled up, and they even picked up 12 baskets of leftover bread and fish. When we feel we have no power, we can hear Him say, "You feed them." Philippians 4:13 (NKJV) "I can do ALL things through Christ who strengthens me." We have THE MIRACLE WORKER, the Creator of the universe, living with, and within us! We may not feel worthy or able, but He says to us, "YOU FEED THEM." We can do this today!

MARK 6:37-44 (NLT)

"Late in the afternoon his disciples came to him and said, "This is a desolate place, and it is getting late. Send the crowds away so they can go to the nearby farms and Villages and buy themselves some food. " but Jesus said, "You feed them." "With what?" They asked." It would take a small fortune to buy food for all this crowd! " "How much food do you have? " He asked. "Go and find out." They came back and reported, " We have five loaves of bread and two fish." Then Jesus told the crowd to sit down in groups on the green grass. So they sat in groups of 50 or 100. Jesus Took The Five Loaves and two fish looked up toward heaven, and asked God's blessing on the food. Breaking the loaves into pieces, he kept giving the bread and fish to the disciples to give to the people. They all ate as much as they wanted, and they picked up 12 baskets of leftover bread and fish. 5,000 men had eaten from those five loaves!" HE is calling out to us the same today, "YOU FEED THEM."

123

God has done great things for each of us! It would be good for us, and bless us, today to take some time and get PERSONAL with OUR GOD and thank Him for specific things He has done in our lives. Praise Him!

1 Samuel 12:24 (NIV)

"But be sure to fear the LORD and serve him faithfully with all your heart; consider what great things he has done for you."

_____

_____

_____

_____

_____

_____

_____

_____

_____

_____

_____

_____

_____

Are we done with chasing this world and its desires yet? Do we take the hand offered to us by Christ Jesus? Do we take it seriously?

1 Peter 4:1-3 (NLT)

"So then, since Christ suffered physical pain, you must arm yourselves with the same attitude he had, and be ready to suffer, too. For if you have suffered physically for Christ, you have finished with sin. You won't spend the rest of your lives chasing your own desires, but you will be anxious to do the will of God. you have had enough in the past of the evil things the godless people enjoy--their immorality and lust, they're feasting and drunkenness and wild parties, and their terrible worship of idols."

_____
_____
_____
_____
_____
_____
_____
_____
_____
_____
_____
_____
_____

What do I do today!? What is my life purpose!? SERVE THE KING! How do we do this?

Matthew 25:40 (NIV)

"The King will reply, 'Truly I tell you, whatever you did for one of the least of these brothers and sisters of Mine, you did for Me.'"

1 Cor 16:15 (NLT) "You know that Stephanus and his household were the first of the harvest of believers in Greece, and they are SPENDING their lives in SERVICE to God's people." "SPENDING THEIR LIVES". We all 'spend our lives' on something. How do we use our God given time on earth? What are we called to do today? "SERVE GOD'S PEOPLE."

_____

_____

_____

_____

_____

_____

_____

_____

_____

_____

_____

126

This is so sweet! No matter how difficult it is, we have this hope. Hell has no hope. We do!

Titus 3:4-7 (NIV)

"But when the kindness and love of God our savior appeared he saved us, not because of righteous things we had done, but because of his Mercy. He saved us through the washing of rebirth and Renewal by the Holy Spirit, whom he poured out on us generously through Jesus Christ Our Savior, so that, having been justified by his grace, we might become heirs having the hope of eternal life."

___
___
___
___
___
___
___
___
___
___
___
___

127

Christians don't lose hope or get frustrated with yourself!

Philippians 2:13 (NLT)

"For God is WORKING IN YOU, giving you the DESIRE and the POWER to do what pleases him."

_____

_____

_____

_____

_____

_____

_____

_____

_____

_____

_____

_____

_____

_____

128

So, you want to go deeper? 1 Cor 6:17 (NKJV), "But he who is joined to the Lord is one spirit with Him." Remember the secret, "Christ w/in you". We are to put on the Lord Jesus. We are required to be holy because God is Holy. You know, the truth is we never will be, no matter how hard we try, or for how many years we try in our own power. We are to put on HIS HOLINESS. We can have that right NOW. Enter in. Embrace what God is doing inside us.

Confident HOPE! Do we feel that powerful stirring inside us of God's peace resting on us and His approval anointing us? Do we actually feel it; feel different? Or, do we just think it may be so, but continue to struggle within ourselves over our identity? Please listen to Paul's prayer for us in ROMANS 15:13 (NLT) " I pray that God, the source of hope, will fill you completely with joy and peace because you trust in him. Then you will overflow with CONFIDENT HOPE through the power of the Holy Spirit."

No, we do not change the way we think, He does! It is not controlled by our actions, words, or thoughts, but rather by His gift to us of, "CONFIDENT HOPE THROUGH the POWER OF THE HOLY SPIRIT." Paul's prayer is that we may live in, and experience, the reality of this CONFIDENT hope today. Peace to all this Christmas.

Life is short whether you live to be 100 or you die young. Live and be thankful in the present day.

_____

_____

_____

_____

_____

_____

_____

_____

_____

_____

_____

_____

_____

_____

_____

_____

_____

_____

131

WE'RE GONNA MAKE IT! Though we may be in the midst of a storm and crashing waves!

Acts 27:23,24 (NIV) "Last night an angel of the God to whom I belong and whom I serve stood beside me 24 and said, 'Do not be afraid, Paul. You must stand trial before Caesar; and God has graciously given you the lives of all who sail with you.'

WE'RE GONNA MAKE IT! Hold on! We will experience this day in Zephaniah 3:17 (ESV)

"The Lord your God is in your midst, a mighty one who will save; he will rejoice over you with gladness; he will quiet you (CALM YOU) by his love; he will exult over you with loud singing."

_____

_____

_____

_____

_____

_____

_____

_____

_____

_____

_____

The Heart of the Father

In my son's football games, I watched him with a passion. I watched every move he made. I even watched him while he was on the sidelines. I felt God tell me today that this is how He watches me too, daily. I told one of my daughters, who is in gymnastics, the other day, "I'm proud of you when you get a high score, but I'm most proud of you when you fall down, or have a not so good performance, but get up and keep going with your head held high." The Father, God, I imagine, watches us this way too. He watches us with passion. We are His children. He cheers when we have our victories. However, He is most proud of us when we are facing a trial, or have just stumbled or failed. Yet, we get back up, keep our head up (we know whose child we are) and move on in trusting in Him all the way.

_____

_____

_____

_____

_____

_____

_____

_____

_____

_____

_____

133

POLITICS EVERYWHERE!! Hope in the world's popularity everywhere!

Although we should boldly stand and do what we can to, spread God's light, bring justice and righteousness, in and through our world's systems, and honor those who do, OUR KINGDOM, is NOT, will not be, now or ever, of this world! It is not based on someone's vote! Do not expect acknowledgement and acceptance from this world. Our true favor, peace and wellbeing is not held in our political governments or democratic hands. Our favor from God and His kingdom is so much bigger! For Christmas let us receive the greatest gift of all.

ISAIAH 9:6,7 (NLT)

"For a child is born to us, a son is given to us. The government will rest on his shoulders. And he will be called WONDERFUL COUNSELOR, MIGHTY GOD, EVERLASTING FATHER, PRINCE OF PEACE. His government and its peace will never end. He will rule with fairness and Justice from the Throne of his ancestor David for all eternity. The passionate commitment of the LORD OF HEAVEN'S ARMIES will make this happen!"

134

Where is the joy in Christianity? It feels as though sometimes the actions of being a Christian, going to church, reading the Bible, doing this and not doing this and that, etc., can become burdensome and tedious. However, GOOD NEWS!!! We are not called to just be members of a social club. True Christianity is not about just following the rules.

Acts 2:28 (NLT) "You have shown me the way of life, and you will fill me with the JOY OF YOUR PRESENCE."

Matthew 1:23 (NIV)

"The virgin will conceive and give birth to a son, and they will call him Immanuel" (which means "God with us")."

Immanuel!!! "God IS with us!" The joy of being a Christian is that God is with us, each of us, inside of us! We cannot run too far, fall too low, or climb too high. His PRESENCE is within us who have received Him and called Him Lord. This is our joy!

_____

_____

_____

_____

_____

_____

_____

_____

_____

135

Welcome to the KINGDOM! Enjoy!

John 18:36 (NLT)

"Jesus answered 'My KINGDOM is not an earthly kingdom. If it were, my followers would fight to keep me from being handed over to the Jewish leaders. But my KINGDOM is not of this world.'"

_____

_____

_____

_____

_____

_____

_____

_____

_____

_____

_____

_____

_____

_____

_____

_____

_____

136

Good News! Have we fallen again? If so, it means we can receive God's grace, again, and again, and again. God's grace, through Who Jesus is and what Jesus did is our strength. God's grace is no different upon our timeline of fallings. But, He will not leave us the same!

John 1:16 (NLT) "From His ABUNDANCE we have ALL received one GRACIOUS blessing after another." Translated in Greek it reads RECEIVED GRACE UPON GRACE). Peace.

_____
_____
_____
_____
_____
_____
_____
_____
_____
_____
_____
_____
_____

We live by the BREATH of God. GEN 2:7 (NLT) "He breathed the breath of life into the man's nostrils, and the man became a living person." THE BREATH OF LIFE!

John 20:22 (NLT) "Then He breathed on them and said, "Receive the Holy Spirit..."

I don't really want to be breathed upon in these virus conscious times. But, when it's the Almighty God Himself, who holds life itself in His hands, I want it and NEED it. Imagine, our resurrected Lord Jesus standing before us and breathing on us, and us receiving, by this breath, the Holy Spirit, actually at that moment, within us. In the NLT, the study notes on John 20:22 in the Life Application Study Bible say, 'God's first breath made man different from all other forms of creation. Through the breath of Jesus, God imparted eternal, spiritual life. With this inbreathing came the power to do God's will on earth.'

Yes Jesus, breath into us Your Holy Spirit, new life and power to rock this world!

Anyone want more hope and bigger expectations in their life? When does a player have the most hope? When the shot is in the air! Want more hope n big expectations...? Take more shots! Yes, listen to the Lord. What actions of faith and love is He putting on your heart? Don't wait for someone else to do it. Take the risk. You're Heavenly Coach is calling out to you, "You're in the open! Be bold! Take the shot!"

What more could we want for Christmas? When asked, "What do you want for Christmas?", there is a yearning in my soul that is hard to express.

Colossians 2:2,3 (NLT)

"I want them to have complete confidence that they understand God's MYSTERIOUS PLAN, which is Christ himself. In Him lie HIDDEN all the TREASURES of wisdom and knowledge."

Do not yield to the popular, but yield to the Word of God and His call on our individual lives. In Jesus time the Jews were awaiting the messiah. They believed that Elijah would be the Messiah's forerunner. They believed John the Baptist was fulfilling that role. So, the Jewish leaders sent priests and Temple assistants to ask him. This was John's chance for popularity.

John 1:19-23 (NLT)

"This was John's testimony when the Jewish leaders sent priests and Temple assistants from Jerusalem to ask John, 'Who are you?' He came right out and said, 'I am NOT the Messiah.' 'Well then, who are you?' They asked. 'Are you Elijah?' 'NO' he replied. 'Are you the prophet we are expecting?' 'NO.' 'Then who are you? We need an answer for those who sent us. What do you have to say about yourself?' John replied in the words of the prophet Isaiah: "I am a voice shouting in the wilderness, 'Clear the way for the Lord's coming!'""

John did not exalt himself when he had the chance. He said he was only who and what God called him to do. Nothing more. So, let us not pursue popularity and/or leaders' acceptance. But, let us NOT remain SILENT through our words or actions when God has called us to speak and act. GOD USES EVERYONE OF US for His glorious purpose and plan if we ALLOW HIM. GOD is speaking to all of us 'John the Baptists' regardless of position or popularity, "NOW CHILDREN! SHINE! SPEAK!"

_____

_____

_____

_____

_____

_____

GOING THROUGH SOME OF LIFE'S CHALLENGES? Why can we be THANKFUL even in our trials? Because our faith must be "worked out in EXPERIENCE." John 1:35-37 (NLT) "The following day John was again standing with two of his disciples. As Jesus walked by, John looked at him and declared, "There is the Lamb of God! " when John's two disciples heard this, they followed Jesus." John the Baptists disciples so easily followed Jesus when John professed that Jesus was the chosen one of God. However, it took several years for their faith to become a deep knowledge of, and gratitude for Jesus. NLT Study Notes, John 1:35 in the Life Application Study Bible ".... What they so easily professed had to be worked out in experience. We may find that words of faith come easily, but deep appreciation for Christ comes with living by faith."

142

Do not forget WHO is with YOU, and WHAT HE has called YOU to do in this world. We are not normal human beings.

Acts 16:18 (NLT) "...'I COMMAND you in the name of JESUS CHRIST to come out of her.' And it instantly left her."

NO, WE ARE NOT NORMAL.

_____

_____

_____

_____

_____

_____

_____

_____

_____

_____

_____

_____

_____

_____

_____

In this life we are called to do things FOR God. It is with His HEART, given to US, that we move forward to give to others what HE PUTS in our heart. We do not do this to get praise from man, though, that may come. We should also not hold back from giving what we have been given because of a false humility. Life is short, let us use our time to RECEIVE from God and GIVE that which has been given.

1Thessalonians 2:4-6 (NLT) "...Our purpose is to please God, not people. He alone examines the motives of our hearts. Never once did we try to win you with flattery, as you well know. And God is our witness that we were not pretending to be your friends just to get your money! As for human praise, we have never sought it from you or anyone else."

PRAY SCRIPTURE. Input a person's name in the verse and make it personal. God knows and hears.

Ezekiel 34:12 (NIV)

"As a shepherd looks after his scattered flock when he is with them, so will I look after my sheep (So too Jesus, look after 'PERSON'S NAME'). I will rescue them (Jesus rescue 'PERSON'S NAME') from all the places where they were scattered on a day of clouds and darkness."

God is GOOD and ALL POWERFUL. He wants too, and WILL, free His children.

_____

_____

_____

_____

_____

_____

_____

_____

_____

_____

_____

_____

_____

DON'T GIVE UP! "SO, LET'S NOT GET TIRED OF DOING WHAT IS GOOD."GALATIANS 6:9 (NLT)

IF WE DONT GIVE UP.................."AT JUST THE RIGHT TIME WE WILL REAP..." GALATIANS 6:9 (NLT). IT'S COMING.

_____

_____

_____

_____

_____

_____

_____

_____

_____

_____

_____

_____

_____

_____

_____

_____

_____

_____

146

"A HARVEST OF BLESSING" GAL 6:9

"THEREFORE, whenever we have the opportunity, we should do good to everyone, especially to those in the family of faith." GAL 6:10 (NLT). SO, BE COMMITED TO A COMMUNITY OF BELIEVERS! DO GOOD TO THEM AND TO OTHERS! DO YOU WANT TO SEE BLESSINGS PIERCE THE DARKNESS?

_____

_____

_____

_____

_____

_____

_____

_____

_____

_____

_____

_____

_____

_____

_____

147

Let our thoughts and feelings of others be based upon what God SEES and not by our human perceptions.

1 Samuel 16:7 (NLT)

"But the Lord said to Samuel, "Don't judge by his appearance or height, for I have rejected him. The Lord doesn't see things the way you see them. People judge by outward appearance, but the Lord looks at the HEART.""

_____

_____

_____

_____

_____

_____

_____

_____

_____

_____

_____

_____

_____

No matter what we may be facing. Here is the summation of all.

Philippians 2:9-11 (NLT)

"Therefore, God elevated him to the place of highest honor and gave him the name ABOVE all other names, that at the name of JESUS EVERY KNEE shall bow, in heaven and on earth and under the earth, and EVERY TONGUE confess that JESUS CHRIST IS LORD, to the glory of GOD THE FATHER."

It is finished.

_____

_____

_____

_____

_____

_____

_____

_____

_____

_____

_____

_____

149

A reminder that we serve our GOD who is so much greater than the things we see in our lives today.

ISAIAH 65:17 (NIV)

17 "See, I will create new heavens and a new earth. The former things will not be remembered, nor will they come to mind."

_____

_____

_____

_____

_____

_____

_____

_____

_____

_____

_____

_____

_____

_____

_____

_____

Isaiah 43:19 (NIV) "19 See, I am doing a new thing! Now it springs up; do you not perceive it? I am making a way in the wilderness and streams in the wasteland."

Wait...! Look for it...Look for it...! God is doing a new work in our lives today! If we EXPECT IT, we will see it! Have faith!

Ephesians 2:8-10 (NIV)

For it is by grace you have been saved through faith, and this not from yourselves; it is the gift of God, 9not by works, so that no one can boast. 10For we are God's workmanship, created in Christ Jesus to do good works, which God prepared in advance as our way of life."

So, EXPECT, HIS WORK in our lives TODAY!

_____

_____

_____

_____

_____

_____

_____

_____

_____

_____

_____

_____

Trust in the Lord's care and working in our life today. HOPE in the Lord and look at what awaits us:

Isaiah 40:30-31 (NIV)

30 Even youths grow tired and weary, and young men stumble and fall; 31 but those who hope in the LORD will renew their strength. They will soar on wings like eagles; they will run and not grow weary, they will walk and not be faint.

_____

_____

_____

_____

_____

_____

_____

_____

_____

_____

_____

_____

_____

152

Our lives can seem like an out of control roller coaster ride. We wait, ready for the inevitable of flying off the rails. Rather, let us choose to take God with us today and...TRUST. Trust, trust. Trust that God is with us. Trust He is watching over us. Trust that He will act to bless us and He will NEVER FAIL us. So, we CAN... give ALL our worries and cares to Him because HE CARES about US.

1 Peter 4:19 (NLT) "So if you are suffering in a manner that pleases God, keep on doing what is right, and trust your lives to the God who created you, for he will never fail you."

1 Peter 5:6,7 (NLT)

"So humble yourselves under the mighty power of God, and at the right time he will lift you up in honor. Give all your worries and cares to God, for He cares about you."

_____

_____

_____

_____

_____

_____

_____

_____

_____

HOLY! Set apart. Sacred and fearful. We are called to God's holiness, yet we are sinners. God calls us a 'royal priesthood'.

1 Peter 2:9 (NIV)

"But you are a chosen people, a royal priesthood, a holy nation, God's special possession, that you may declare the praises of him who called you out of darkness into his wonderful light."

Yet, we sin. The Holy Spirit is associated with Holiness. Jesus is not referred to as 'Holy Jesus' or God the Father as, 'Holy Father' when we speak of the Trinity, but the Holy Spirit is the Holy Spirit. That 'Holy' can refer to what He is doing in us. He is continuously working out our sanctification; our holiness. Now we are called the 'Temple of the Holy Spirit'. His work is sanctifying us. We are called to be 'holy', to be set apart and pure. Yet, we come up short. Grace! Step by step the Holy Spirit is on the job working out our sanctification, transforming us. Now, being a royal priesthood, we can come directly into God's presence. We don't need a human priest to go into the presence of God for us. We all are the priests. This is the great work God has done. We, each of us, are the temple of the presence, of the Holy Spirit, of God.

Colossians 1:26,27 (NIV)

"26 the mystery that has been kept hidden for ages and generations but is now disclosed to the Lord's people. 27To them God has chosen to make known among the Gentiles the glorious riches of this mystery, which is Christ IN YOU, the hope of glory."

Have peace and grace today. Do not give up. God's Holy Spirit work is not done with us yet. But, our position is to come into His presence, by what Jesus did for us, and allow the Holy Spirit to transform us, even the way we think, TODAY. Yes, there is hope. We can be changed.

_____

_____

_____

154

Urgent message:

RECEIVE HIS LOVE TODAY! We are commanded by Jesus to love one another as He loves us.

1 John 3:23 (NLT)

And this is His commandment: We must believe in the name of his Son, Jesus Christ, and love one another, just as He commanded us."

However, let us please remember where this love begins. We don't receive God's love BECAUSE we love others (our actions). Rather, we love others BECAUSE He FIRST loved (we receive) us. We need to receive daily God's love for US to bring His love to others. We must live in the DIVINE power of His love for us and others. We cannot conjure up within ourselves this love He is calling us to have for others. On my own, my love is deplete.

1 John 4:19 (NLT)

"We love each other because He loved us first."

So, daily we must be renewed in the Spirit to live this powerful life of love. It is so otherworldly beyond ourselves.

_____

_____

_____

_____

_____

_____

_____

155

Preach, teach, listen to, be changed by, the whole biblical gospel, right?

1 Peter 3:6 (NLT)

"for instance, Sarah obeyed her husband, Abraham, and called him her master. You are her daughters when you do what is right without FEAR of what your husband's might do."

This doesn't refer to not fearing an abusive husband, but rather the fear of putting a wife's trust in believing in God's revelation, work, and leadership that God is doing in a wife's husbands' life. It is speaking to the releasing of control that a wife may want to take regarding her husband's actions. It is trusting God's work and will in her husband's life so that she will not try to control this, God work, process. In verse 5 it states, "This is how the holy women of old made themselves beautiful." Let us see the beauty, and the releasing of God's power through this. "YOUR kingdom come! YOUR will be done ('in my husband's life'-example of worded prayer), on earth as it is in heaven." The releasing of a wives attempted control over her husband, and trusting in God's work with him, not her own work with him, allows the power, freedom and flow of God's work to happen. It releases the husband and the wife unto God's power and enhances the relationship of the two. It is what both, wife and husband, always wanted. Trust God's working with your spouse.

156

True life today, comes from the reality of these words.

1 Peter 2:22-25 (NLT)

"He never sinned, nor ever deceived anyone. He did not retaliate when he was insulted, nor threaten revenge when he suffered. He left his case in the hands of God, who always judges fairly. He personally carried our sins in His body on the cross so that we can be dead to sin and live for what is right. By his wounds you are healed. Once you were like sheep who wandered away. But now you have turned to your Shepherd, the Guardian of your souls."

_____

_____

_____

_____

_____

_____

_____

_____

_____

_____

369 Who am I in Christ today? Am I still acceptable, approved, and have His presence working in and through me? Here's a few things the Word says:

Lamentations 3:22 (NIV)

"Because of the LORD's great love, we are not consumed, for his compassions never fail."

1 JOHN 2:12-14 (NLT)

"I am writing to you who are God's children because YOUR SINS HAVE BEEN FORGIVEN through Jesus. I am writing to you who are mature in the faith because YOU KNOW CHRIST, who existed from the beginning. I am writing to you who are young in the faith because YOU HAVE WON your battle with the evil one. I have written to you who are God's children because YOU KNOW the Father. I have written to you who are mature in the faith because YOU KNOW CHRIST, who existed from the beginning. I have written to you who are young in the faith because YOU ARE STRONG. God's word lives in your heart's, and YOU HAVE WON your battle with the evil one."

If we question our strength or position with Christ because of how we may be feeling weak or unworthy, we are wrong. Listen again to the above message from John, "The disciple Christ loved.", and see what He really thinks of each of us. Let us go, wherever today, with our heads lifted up because He is with us! The enemy says we are not, God says "We are."

_____

_____

_____

_____

_____

"God, I feel judged by you. I continue to do too many wrong actions to receive Your love and approval. I am not worthy.", I said.

"Who told you that!?", God replied.

Who keeps telling us we are too far away, or too fallen, to receive God's amazing love and mercy?

Lamentations 3:22, 23 (NIV)

22 "Because of the Lord's great love we are not consumed, for his compassions never fail. 23 They are new every morning; great is your faithfulness."

"Give thanks to the God of heaven. His love endures forever" (Psalm 136:26).

1 John 4:19 (NIV)

"We love because he first loved us."

_____

_____

_____

_____

_____

_____

_____

_____

_____

Philippians 4:4 (NIV) "Rejoice in the Lord always."

Philippians 1:25 (NLT) "...so I can continue to help all of you grow and experience the joy of your faith."

Sounds like joy for a Christian is a commandment. If we don't have it we are overcome by a form of the flesh and are in sin. Joy is a decision, not always a state of happiness, or being. It is beautiful, that as Christ followers, we are free to make that choice. God is ALWAYS good to His children! Let us choose JOY today.

_____

_____

_____

_____

_____

_____

_____

_____

_____

_____

_____

_____

_____

_____

_____

_____

160# 160

Every Word out of Jesus mouth is worth loving, and also mind shifting. He is God Himself speaking to us.

LUKE 18:14 (NLT) ".... For those who exalt themselves will be humbled, and those who humble themselves will be exalted."

He is a light to our daily path.

_____

_____

_____

_____

_____

_____

_____

_____

_____

_____

_____

_____

_____

_____

161

God's loving and being inside us, can we hear it? Are we listening? His love runs deep. Receive and change. Be the person he has created. Allow the Holy Spirit to change even the way we think. Allow him to give us joy, peace, patience, hope, courage, and boldness. This is Who We Are. God is good. This is his gift to his children. So, no more fear, worry, or anxiety. He is with us. So, let him do it. Stop trying to do it through our old man/woman. He/she is already dead. Stop trying to make your flesh acceptable. It is dead. Allow your spirit to soar.

162

We seem to live in a world wrought with chaos. We may even experience a form of chaos intruding into our own personal lives through relationships, business, health, etc.... What will our future be with all this unsteadiness?

Psalm 37:37 (NIV)

"Consider the blameless, observe the upright; a FUTURE awaits those who SEEK PEACE."

_____

_____

_____

_____

_____

_____

_____

_____

_____

_____

_____

_____

_____

_____

163

Rejoice! Rejoice and experience the newness of our relationship with God in the NOW. GOD'S KINGDOM IS 'NOW', WITHIN US!!!!!!

Luke 17:20,21 (NKJV)

Now when He was asked by the Pharisees when the kingdom of God would come, He answered them and said, "The Kingdom of God does not come with observation; nor will they say, 'See here!' or 'See there!' For indeed, the kingdom of God is within you."

164

This morning as I hold the Bible in my hands I see it as an ocean; vast and diverse. Yet, it is all one. We can dive into it whenever we want and experience the riches that God has waiting for us. Like God's ocean and His created nature within this world, He has put within it elements of healing for our bodies. So too, this Bible, this ocean, has Words of healing for our souls and spirits throughout it. As we dive in daily, we can go on a God led guided tour, and partake of His beauty and healing powers daily. These Words are the beginning.

Proverbs 3:5-6 (NIV)

5 "Trust in the LORD with all your heart and lean not on your own understanding; 6 in all your ways submit to him, and he will make your paths straight."

_____
_____
_____
_____
_____
_____
_____
_____
_____
_____
_____

165

I feel like maybe I am opening Pandora's box. But, SUICIDE? Why would one think of suicide if they had this below?

Psalm 3:2-6 (NIV)

"Many are saying of me, "God will not deliver him." 3 But you, LORD, are a shield around me, my glory, the One who lifts my head high. 4 I call out to the LORD, and he answers me from his holy mountain. 5 I lie down and sleep; I wake again, because the LORD sustains me. 6 I will not fear though tens of thousands assail me on every side."

166

Here is GOD'S word of encouragement to us. Know that we have an awesome God on our side who loves us and even fights our battles. We are not alone.

"What, then, shall we say in response to these things? If God is for us, who can be against us?"

Romans 8:31 (NIV)

_____

_____

_____

_____

_____

_____

_____

_____

_____

_____

_____

_____

_____

_____

Is the 'terrible day' of the Lord near? In ancient times this prophecy did already get fulfilled when Babylon invaded the land, but many believe this prophecy has a double fulfillment-one for the Old Testament times and one for end time prophecy.

Zephaniah 1:14 (NLT)

"That terrible day of the Lord is near. Swiftly it comes-"

That terrible day when God will, because He is holy, 'actively judge and justly punish everyone who is CONTENT to live in sin, indifferent to Him, or unconcerned about justice.'

Jesus have mercy!

_____

_____

_____

_____

_____

_____

_____

_____

_____

_____

_____

168

Being strong can be a sacrifice to the Lord. Sometimes we may want to hide in our cave and let the world go by. Sometimes we may not feel strong simply because when we ask Him for strength we are asking for our own personal selfish reasons like not feeling inferior, insecure or like we may be perceiving others supposed strength and we want to be like them. We ask but we do not receive because we are asking for strength based upon selfish purposes. If you want strength then fall into it based upon His WILL and PURPOSE for your life. Sacrifice our own feelings and desires of strength and receive His own WILL for our strength today. He wants us divinely superpowered with HIS STRENGTH today. Receive it and put it on today. The bible says, "My grace is all you need. My power works best in weakness." 2 Corinthians 12:9 (NLT). So, put on, walk in, His strength of the Holy Spirit presence within us today. Our weakness leads to strength. We do not remain weak. Let His Spirit transform us, even the way we think!

_____

_____

_____

_____

_____

_____

_____

_____

_____

_____

169

Strength is there for us TODAY because our God LIVES.

Habakkuk 3:16-19 (NLT)

"I will wait quietly for the coming day when disaster will strike the people who invade us. Even though the fig trees have no blossoms, and there are no grapes on the vines; even though the olive crop fails, and the fields lie empty and barren; even though the flocks die in the fields, and the cattle barns are empty, yet I will rejoice in the Lord! I will be joyful in the God of my salvation! The Sovereign Lord is my strength! He makes me as sure-footed as a deer, able to tread upon the heights."

MAKE NO MISTAKE! When we share God's Word we are not just sharing a belief system, or philosophy. Rather, we are speaking life to death, light into darkness. We are making demons flee at the sound of His voice. His Words are words of life changing, reality altering, POWER.

_____

_____

_____

_____

_____

_____

_____

_____

_____

_____

_____

_____

_____

_____

_____

_____

171

The other part about Jesus taking us by the hand that I forgot this morning is very important to hear. It is that He gives us His COURAGE, His courage to take on whatever lies before us on this very day. Jesus bless you, and grasp His courage in you today.....When we let Him take us by the hand he puts us in our proper position as His children, established in His love, secure in His love for us, and, He gives us His, "God is with me" Courage to face anything before me on this very day.

_____

_____

_____

_____

_____

_____

_____

_____

_____

_____

_____

_____

_____

_____

_____

Please take courage! God has a plan for each of our lives. Yes, it is a glorious, wonderful plan! So, let us lay 'our wills' daily into His will, and hands, and trust Him for the greatest plan of all to happen in our lives.

Galatians 1:15,16 (NLT)

"But even BEFORE I was born, God CHOSE ME and called me by His Marvelous Grace. Then it pleased him to reveal his Son to me so that I would proclaim the good news about Jesus to the Gentiles."

_____

_____

_____

_____

_____

_____

_____

_____

_____

_____

_____

_____

_____

_____

173

God's plan for us in this life: make us HOLY.

ROMANS 6:19 (NLT)

"...Now you must give yourselves to be slaves to righteous living so that you will become HOLY."

Let Him fill every area of our lives. Let our lives, be HIS."

_____

_____

_____

_____

_____

_____

_____

_____

_____

_____

_____

_____

_____

174

The daily drudge..., or

Acts 1:3 (NLT) "..., he appeared to the apostles from time to time, and he proved to them in many ways that he was actually alive. And he talked to them about the KINGDOM OF GOD."

ACTS 1:5 (NLT)

"John baptized with water, but in just a few days you will be baptized with the Holy Spirit."

Let us remember John the Baptists words, "I baptize with water, but the one is coming who will baptize with FIRE."

Though, at times, we may feel we are in a day of drudgery, the Kingdom of God, another world, exists in us, and around us daily too. Yes, God's passion and fire awaits us daily if we but ask and receive.

_____

_____

_____

_____

_____

_____

_____

_____

_____

_____

Trials. We go through them, not so that we will be people with more bumps and bruises. We are not His beat up chosen ones. But rather, we are His flames! We are called to burn today!

"He announced, 'I indeed baptize you with water unto repentance, but He who is coming after me is mightier than I, whose sandals I am not worthy to carry. He will baptize you with the Holy Spirit and FIRE.' " Matthew 3:11 (NKJV)

176

Wait for it! Wait for it! It's the...new trial!

We don't know when they will come, what form, and to what degree, but we know, being part of life, they will come.

Isaiah 26:3 (NIV)

"3 You will keep in perfect peace those whose minds are steadfast, because they trust in you."

PERFECT peace. Being perfect, this peace overrules anything this world brings against us. STEADFAST speaks of an unmovable loyalty and faith in our MINDS. 'TRUST in YOU', leads us to the Lord's prayer when we are told by God, Jesus, to pray, "YOUR Kingdom come, YOUR will be done, on earth as it is in heaven." This prayer is not just for the world, in general, but is for each of our daily lives. God is good. He loves and pursues His children.

_____

_____

_____

_____

_____

_____

_____

_____

_____

_____

James 4:2-4 (NLT) "... Yet you don't have what you want because you don't ask God for it. And even when you ask, you don't get it because your motives are all wrong--you want only what will give you pleasure. You adulterers! Don't you realize that friendship with the world makes you an enemy of God? I say it again: if you want to be a friend of the world, you make yourself an enemy of God."

We read this and think, "This isn't referring to me... is it?"

God, thank You for your mercy on me. More please.

178

What things or, a thing, do we feel God has called us to in this life? What is our vision. At times, we may feel it cannot happen. But, do not be daunted! He is with us, and, by His power, He will make it happen!

Isaiah 41:10 (NIV)

"10 So do not fear, for I am with you; do not be dismayed, for I am your God. I will strengthen you and help you; I will uphold you with my righteous right hand."

No fear my brothers and sisters!

_____

_____

_____

_____

_____

_____

_____

_____

_____

_____

_____

_____

179

Galatians 5:13 (NLT)

"For you have been called to live in freedom, my brothers and sisters.... Instead, use your freedom to serve one another in love."

What God considers freedom, and what we consider freedom, are not up for debate with our human minds. It is experiential, and is beyond our human way of thinking. When we are 'set free' beyond our human analysis and thoughts, we are able to experience, through the Spirit, the glorious, life altering, reality of God's WORD. We become slayed, gloriously transformed into a NEW REALITY where we are FREE to 'love our neighbor as ourself.' Let us not be 'Christian' thinkers, but rather 'Christian' TRANSFORMATIONS.

180

This is a tie in with the last message received about Jesus showing His Godly AUTHORITY while He walked this earth, and now, He amazingly lives in us.

Today... God talks about the incredible POWER there is for those who believe in Him. Ephesians 1:19-23 (NLT)

"I also pray that you will understand the incredible greatness of GOD'S POWER for US who believe in him. This is the same MIGHTY POWER that raised Christ from the dead and seated him in the place of honor at God's right hand in the heavenly realms. Now he is far above any ruler or authority or power or leader or anything else-- not only in this world but ALSO in the WORLD

TO COME. God has put ALL THINGS under the authority of Christ and has made him head over all things for the benefit of the church. And the church is His body, it is made full and complete by Christ, who fills all things everywhere with himself." Let us allow the Holy Spirit to fill us with Christ today.

_____

_____

_____

_____

_____

_____

_____

_____

_____

Who is this Son of Man, Jesus? The boat is sinking. The disciples frantically wake him up, shouting, "Teacher, don't you even care that we are going to drown?" Then, when he woke he rebuked the wind and said to the water, "QUIET DOWN!" Immediately, the wind stopped and there was a great calm! Then, there was the demon possessed man who had a legion of demons within him. Jesus tells them to leave and they complied. The crowds came to see the man because he was now fully sane. Who is this SON OF MAN who has so much authority that even nature and demons immediately obey him? Who are we? This same SON OF MAN now lives IN US! Colossians 1:27 (NLT)

"...And this is the secret: CHRIST LIVES IN YOU..."

Let us run with this! It is not only the amazing power and authority, it is also the amazing LOVE within us to receive and also give to others. PEACE

_____

_____

_____

_____

_____

_____

_____

_____

_____

_____

182

This world, what does it offer us? What do we seek from it? Do we seek comfort, status, physical pleasure, emotional needs in relationships? What? What are we doing with this short time we have been given here on this earth? Are we seeking the temporary or the ETERNAL?

While in his human body walking this earth, Jesus performed a huge miracle. There were 5 thousand people that needed to be fed, and he fed them all, and there were baskets full of leftovers, with five barley loaves and two fish that a young boy had. It looks like He did this to show the people he was their Savior who came to bring eternal freedom and life. After this, the large crowd followed him. He rebuked them though, saying they were only following him because he gave them food. Today, why are we following Jesus. Are we following him for what we believe he will give us in this life, or are we laying this life down to receive eternal life, no matter the cost, and follow him into His Kingdom. What do we seek!?

John 6:26,27 (NLT)

"Jesus replied, "I tell you the truth, you want to be with me because I fed you, not because you understood the miraculous signs. But don't be so concerned about perishable things like food. Spend your energy seeking the eternal life that the Son of Man can give you. For God the Father has given me the seal of his approval."

_____

_____

_____

_____

_____

_____

We are known by, called by, changed by, and owned by Jesus. We think we may know ourselves, but we really don't. We are created by Jesus and are fully known by Him.

John 1:42 (NLT) "Then Andrew brought Simon to meet Jesus. Looking intently at Simon, Jesus said, 'You are Simon, the son of John-- but you will be called Cephas.'"

Jesus already knows us and tells us who we really are. Later, in the same chapter in verse 46-49 we hear, " Philip went off to look for Nathaniel and told him, 'We have found the very person Moses and the prophets wrote about! His name is Jesus, the son of Joseph from Nazareth.' 'Nazareth!' exclaimed Nathaniel. 'Can anything good come from there?' 'Just come and see for yourself.' Philip said. As they approached, Jesus said, 'Here comes an honest man-- a true son of Israel'. 'How do you know about me?' Nathaniel asked. And Jesus replied, "I could see you under the fig tree before Philip found you."

Today, we have both the Spirit and the flesh trying to tell us who we are. Let us choose to hear from Jesus who we truly are today.

_____

_____

_____

_____

_____

_____

_____

_____

184

Do we truly desire the Holy Spirits power manifest in our lives?

Then we must not only ask for and believe, but we must OBEY Him.

Acts 5:32 (NLT)

"We are witnesses of these things and so is the Holy Spirit, who is GIVEN BY GOD to those who OBEY him."

_____

_____

_____

_____

_____

_____

_____

_____

_____

_____

_____

_____

_____

185

"Is ANYTHING too hard for the Lord?"

This was spoken by God to Abraham when his wife Sarah laughed at the Lord's words that Sarah would be having a baby in about a year. Abraham and Sarah were very old. I love how God was so personal with them and how He knew them and their futures.

What about us today? When we feel God has given us promises, but we feel we're too old now, or that it is too late due to some fault of ours, do we feel God cannot work in and through us now too? Let us not give up on ourselves. In doing so, we are giving up on God.

Genesis 18:13-15 (NLT)

"Then the Lord said to Abraham, 'Why did Sarah laugh? Why did she say, can an old woman like me have a baby? IS ANYTHING TOO HARD FOR THE LORD? About a year from now, just as I told you, I will return, and Sarah will have a son.' Sarah was afraid, so she denied that she had laughed. But he said, 'That is not true you did laugh.' " It is so personal. The truth is so important that He even calls Sarah out on not being true in her words. The truth is not our feelings, but, rather, His Word- His promises.

_____

_____

_____

_____

_____

_____

_____

_____

186

WHO ARE YOU?! Who are we?! We are, "his holy people who are his rich and glorious inheritance."

Do we feel holy? No?

Well, we are! Its because of what he did and what he said. He is Lord Almighty. We are not. Let us receive today what He said.

Ephesians 1:18 (NLT)

"I pray that your hearts will be flooded with light so that you can understand the confident hope he has given to those he called--his holy people who are his rich and glorious inheritance."

_____

_____

_____

_____

_____

_____

_____

_____

_____

_____

_____

_____

187

"G R A C E" Let us not read this word as we can sometimes do as we let it fly over our head as we say in our minds, "Yeah, yeah, yeah! I've heard that word many times. Boring!" To the person stumbling into the gates of hell 'grace' is everything, undeserved favor and forgiveness from God. In hell, I don't think there is any more offer of grace. The door is closed for eternity. But, today, with this breath still in us, we have this enormous offer directly from God. It is the power we must rely on daily. God's grace. Favor. Undeserved.

Ephesians 2:8-10 (NLT)

"God saved you by His GRACE when you BELIEVED. And you can't take credit for this; it is a GIFT from God. Salvation is not a reward for the good things we have done, so none of us can boast about it. For we are God's MASTERPIECE. He has created us ANEW in Christ Jesus, so WE CAN DO the GOOD THINGS he PLANNED FOR US long ago."

_____

_____

_____

_____

_____

_____

_____

_____

_____

_____

188

WHAT...? As Christians, do we really believe in?!!

Acts 13:38-40 (NLT)

"Brothers, LISTEN! We are here to Proclaim that through this man JESUS there is FORGIVENESS for your sins. EVERYONE who BELIEVES in HIM is declared RIGHT with God--something the law of Moses could never do. Be careful! Don't let the prophets words apply to you for they said, 'Look, you mockers, be amazed and die! For I am doing something in your own day, something you wouldn't believe even if someone told you about it.'"

_____
_____
_____
_____
_____
_____
_____
_____
_____
_____
_____
_____
_____

God didn't always do the same miracle or style of doing the miracle when he walked this earth. Now we hear the church preach that back in the 60's & 70's God used the youth to bring revival. So, the 'so called' prophets and the church preaches again, "This is how God works. He is going to use the youth to bring revival. When I see a God who one time put mud in a person's eyes to heal them, and then another time saying a person is healed when the person was not even in His presence, I would not want to preach that God is going to do the same movement as before. Let us wake up to the Spirit. The Spirit does not always move as we expect. We cannot put Him in a bottle and patent it.

190

We are called by God, today, to not be led by trauma, worldly pleasures, or anything other the world can produce, but rather we have an urgent call upon our lives today. The call, by Him, is to come into His REST today. Stop being mugged by the world! We are called to LISTEN to the VOICE of God.

Hebrews 4:1-3 (NLT)

"God's promise of entering his REST still stands, so we ought to tremble with fear that some of you might fail to experience it. For this is good news- that God has prepared this rest- has been announced to us just as it was to them. But it did them no good because they didn't share the faith of those who LISTEN to God. For only we who believe can enter his rest...." In verse 7 it says from the words of David, "TODAY when you hear His voice, don't harden your hearts." His voice that we are called to hear today is His word. Verse 12,13 says, "For the word of God is alive and Powerful. It is sharper than the sharpest two-edged sword, cutting between soul and spirit, between joint and marrow. It exposes our innermost thoughts and desires. Nothing in all creation is hidden from God. Everything is naked and exposed before His eyes, and He is the one to whom we are accountable."

So, He is calling us to hear His voice daily. God's rest is there for us to enter today. We are accountable to enter in and hear His voice. We enter it through His word. His word, His kingdom, is a requirement to CHANGE our world's. His word, His voice, is a Holy place of rest.

TODAY!!! Let us enter into His presence and Kingdom and hear from our loving Father, when? Tomorrow? No! TODAY!!!

The bible says this! Check it out!

Hebrews 3:14,15 (NLT)

"For if we are faithful to the end, trusting God just as firmly as when we first believed, we will share in all that belongs to Christ.

Remember what it says:

'TODAY when you HEAR His VOICE, don't harden your hearts as Israel did when they rebelled.'"

TODAY. Let's go in and find out what awaits us in His presence today!

"When we BELONG to GOD, we need NOT fear death, because we know that DEATH is only the DOORWAY into eternal LIFE."

NLT Life Application Study Bible

"... and only by dying could he break the power of the devil, who had the power of death. Only in this way could he set free all who have lived their lives as slaves to the fear of dying." Hebrews 2:14,15 (NLT)

GOOD NEWS! Let us believe and trust. We are not far from home.

God's word is so POWERFUL that the enemy will use any and all means, and thoughts, to keep us away from it! Do NOT let this happen! Come unto the word covered by the Blood of the Lamb and receive His mercy and grace. Have our robes washed. Then enter in and eat from the tree of life.

Revelation 22:14 (NLT)

"Blessed are those who wash their robes. They will be permitted to enter in through the gates of the city and eat the fruit from the tree of life." This scripture may be for a future time but I believe it is also for us today. "Why so downcast, 'O my soul?' ", when He told me to 'COME!'

REV 22:17 (NLT) "The Spirit and the bride say, 'Come.' Let anyone who hears this say, 'Come.' Let anyone who is thirsty come. Let anyone who desires drink freely from the water of life."

_____

_____

_____

_____

_____

193

What are the LAST words, what is the LAST sentence of God's word, in the Bible? All of God's words are important, but do we think that God's last written word's may be of extra importance?

They are words that we all must stand on and live every day.

For, who are we, but all His children, working out our salvation, and going from glory to glory. We are a work in process, relying upon the last words of the Bible as our highest ground in which we stand.

REVELATION 22:21 (NLT)

"MAY THE GRACE OF THE LORD JESUS BE WITH GOD'S HOLY PEOPLE."

_____

_____

_____

_____

_____

_____

_____

_____

_____

_____

_____

_____

In what we are lead to do by Him, and thus, what we do for Him, is glorious. No matter, small or big, what we do today, can be glorious. The Divine One lives in and through us. All glory to Jesus. We shine!

Romans 8:17 (NLT)

"And since we are his children, we are his heirs. In fact, together with Christ we are heirs of God's glory. But if we are to share his glory, we must also share his suffering."

_____

_____

_____

_____

_____

_____

_____

_____

_____

_____

_____

_____

_____

195

Revelations 1:5,6 (NLT)

"...and the ruler of all the kings of the world.

All glory to him who loves us and has freed us from our sins by the shedding of his blood for us. He has made us a kingdom of priests for God his Father." Look what he has done for us! Receive it and function in it! This is his position and our true position because of him. Let us ride in the truth fellow children! Do not be afraid of any of the earth's rulers stirring up destruction. Our king Jesus rules them.

And, joyously, we all receive:

"For from [Christ's] fullness we have all received, grace upon grace" (John 1:16, ESV). Abundance of His grace, grace upon grace. It is not just a one-time thing; we live and breadth in it.

Have we fallen again, or are we feeling like we are in a continuos fall? Are we feeling unlovable by God, judged by God, that His anger surely must be upon us? Well, that's not what Jesus came for. He did not come to condemn us, but to give us abundant life. When we fall, and we carry this load, unconfessed, we put ourselves in a ZONE that Satan wants us in; a place where we seem to be untouchable by the Father's love; a place where we are unworthy to even share His love with others. Here is God's truth:

1 Thessalonians 5:9-11 (NLT)

"For God CHOSE to SAVE US through our Lord Jesus Christ, not to pour out HIS ANGER on us. Christ died for us so that, whether we are dead or alive when he returns, we can live with Him forever. So encourage each other and build each other up, just as you are already doing."

_____

_____

_____

_____

_____

_____

_____

_____

_____

_____

_____

197

Daniel 10:12 (NIV)

12 "Then he continued, 'Do not be afraid, Daniel. Since the first day that you set your mind to gain understanding and to humble yourself before your God, your words were heard, and I have come in response to them.'"

While we live in sick and chaotic times, there are some truths and realities we may easily forget.

God is literally watching over us individually. Not only is He watching us, but He is also protecting, and acting on our behalf. "Do not be afraid, Daniel."

We each have a life calling, God's plan for our lives. When we seek His ways for our lives and humbly submit to His, 'greater than ours' ways, He is there taking control and powerfully changing our lives for our good. Also, He is really listening to each of us. As humans, don't we all really want someone to actually 'listen' to us? Well, here it is. Even better than any human could do. When He says, 'Come!' We should be running and jumping on His lap. He is our loving heavenly Father who wants to provide for His children today.

198

TRUST. The key to God's power!

1 Peter 4:19 (NLT)

"..., and trust your lives to the God who created you, for He will never fail you."

Trust leads us to say, "Whatever mess I'm in, my heavenly Father will bring me through, and He will also make me thrive in and through it."

_____

_____

_____

_____

_____

_____

_____

_____

_____

_____

_____

_____

Whatever trials we are going through here is God's word to us: 2 Peter 3:18 (NLT)

"Rather, you must grow in the GRACE and KNOWLEDGE of our Lord and Savior Jesus Christ. All glory to Him, both now and forever! Amen."

_____

_____

_____

_____

_____

_____

_____

_____

_____

_____

_____

_____

_____

_____

_____

_____

_____

God's word is food that we spiritually and bodily need today. You can call it real SOUL food. We may not be partaking of it because we may not know we NEED this food or we just don't open up the door and let it in. It is strength and joy to our beings, and is a connection with the DIVINE. Like nutritious food that flows through our bodies and makes them strong, so too does His word allow the divine healing and strength to flow through us. Let's open up His word and see what He has on the menu for us today.

_____

_____

_____

_____

_____

_____

_____

_____

_____

_____

_____

_____

_____

_____

Sounds like that when we make the decision to become followers of Jesus we sign up for a hardcore bootcamp. We do not sign up for a life of ease and comfort. Why do we get surprised when there are hardships and trials? But, He/we shall prevail! We are made for this. Hoorah!!!

1 Peter 4:12,13 (NLT)

"Dear friends, don't be surprised at the fiery trials you are going through, as if something strange were happening to you. Instead, be very glad--for these trials make you partners with Christ in his suffering, so that you will have the wonderful joy of seeing his glory when it is revealed to all the world."

202

Let us seek and learn to know this Person better.

1 Peter 3:22 (NLT)

"Now Christ has gone to heaven. He is seated in the place of honor next to God, and all the angels and authorities and powers accept his authority."

Whose authority and friendship do we want to carry with us today?

_____

_____

_____

_____

_____

_____

_____

_____

_____

_____

_____

_____

_____

_____

203

We long to be safely home. God is our ultimate HOME and we are on the way. We have already got the ticket and are on the journey. Might be some bumps along the way, but we have His promise to get us HOME SAFELY. So, let's buckle up and thrive through the ride.

1 Peter 3:18 (NLT)

"Christ suffered for our sins once for all time. He never sinned, but he died for sinners to bring you SAFELY HOME to God...."

Trust in the Lord's care and working in our life today. HOPE in the Lord and look at what awaits us:

Isaiah 40:30-31 (NIV)

30 Even youths grow tired and weary, and young men stumble and fall; 31 but those who hope in the LORD will renew their strength. They will soar on wings like eagles; they will run and not grow weary, they will walk and not be faint.

_____

_____

_____

_____

_____

_____

_____

_____

_____

_____

_____

_____

205

Our lives can seem like an out of control roller coaster ride. We wait, ready for the inevitable of flying off the rails. Rather, let us choose to take God with us today and... TRUST. Trust, trust. Trust that God is with us. Trust He is watching over us. Trust that He will act to bless us and He will NEVER FAIL us. So, we CAN... give ALL our worries and cares to Him because HE CARES about US.

1 Peter 4:19 (NLT)

"So, if you are suffering in a manner that pleases God, keep on doing what is right, and trust your lives to the God who created you, for he will never fail you."

1 Peter 5:6,7 (NLT)

"So, humble yourselves under the mighty power of God, and at the right time he will lift you up in honor. Give all your worries and cares to God, for He cares about you."

_____

_____

_____

_____

_____

_____

_____

_____

_____

HOLY! Set apart. Sacred and fearful. We are called to God's holiness, yet we are sinners. God calls us a 'Royal Priesthood'.

1 Peter 2:9 (NIV)

"But you are a chosen people, a royal priesthood, a holy nation, God's special possession, that you may declare the praises of him who called you out of darkness into his wonderful light."

Yet, we sin. The Holy Spirit is associated with Holiness. Jesus is not referred to as 'Holy Jesus' or God the Father as, 'Holy Father' when we speak of the Trinity, but the Holy Spirit is the Holy Spirit. That 'Holy' can refer to what He is doing in us. He is continuously working out our sanctification; our holiness. Now we are called the 'Temple of the Holy Spirit'. His work is sanctifying us. We are called to be 'holy', to be set apart and pure. Yet, we come up short. Grace! Step by step the Holy Spirit is on the job working out our sanctification, transforming us. Now, being a royal priesthood, we can come directly into God's presence. We don't need a human priest to go into the presence of God for us. We all are the priests. This is the great work God has done. We, each of us, are the temple of the presence, of the Holy Spirit, of God.

2 Colossians 11:26,27 (BSB)

"26 the mystery that was hidden for ages and generations but is now revealed to His saints. 27 To them God has chosen to make known among the Gentiles the glorious riches of this mystery, which is Christ IN YOU, the hope of glory."

Have peace and grace today. Do not give up. God's Holy Spirit work is not done with us yet. But, our position is to come into His presence, by what Jesus did for us, and allow the Holy Spirit to transform us, even the way we think, TODAY. Yes, there is hope. We can be changed.

_____

_____

_____

Urgent message:

RECEIVE HIS LOVE TODAY! We are commanded by Jesus to love one another as He loves us.

1 John 3:23 (NLT)

And this is His commandment: We must believe in the name of his Son, Jesus Christ, and love one another, just as He commanded us."

However, let us please remember where this love begins. We don't receive God's love BECAUSE we love others (our actions). Rather, we love others BECAUSE He FIRST loved (we receive) us. We need to receive daily God's love for US to bring His love to others. We must live in the DIVINE power of His love for us and others. We cannot conjure up within ourselves this love He is calling us to have for others. On my own, my love is incomplete.

1 John 4:19 (NLT)

"We love each other because He loved us first."

So, daily we must be renewed in the Spirit to live this powerful life of love. It is so otherworldly beyond ourselves.

208

Preach, teach, listen to, be changed by, the whole biblical gospel, right?

1 Peter 3:6 (NLT)

"for instance, Sarah obeyed her husband, Abraham, and called him her master. You are her daughters when you do what is right without FEAR of what your husband's might do."

This doesn't refer to not fearing an abusive husband, but rather the fear of putting a wife's trust in believing in God's revelation, work, and leadership that God is doing in a wife's husbands' life. It is speaking to the releasing of control that a wife may want to take regarding her husband's actions. It is trusting God's work and will in her husband's life so that she will not try to control this, God work, process. In verse 5 it states, "This is how the holy women of old made themselves beautiful." Let us see the beauty, and the releasing of God's power through this. "YOUR kingdom come! YOUR will be done ('in my husband's life'-example of worded prayer), on earth as it is in heaven." The releasing of a wives attempted control over her husband, and trusting in God's work with him, not her own work with him, allows the power, freedom and flow of God's work to happen. It releases the husband and the wife unto God's power and enhances the relationship of the two. It is what both, wife and husband, always wanted. Trust God's working with your spouse.

_____

_____

_____

_____

_____

_____

209

True life today, comes from the reality of these words.

1 Peter 2:22-25 (NLT)

"He never sinned, nor ever deceived anyone. He did not retaliate when he was insulted, nor threaten revenge when he suffered. He left his case in the hands of God, who always judges fairly. He personally carried our sins in His body on the cross so that we can be dead to sin and live for what is right. By his wounds you are healed. Once you were like sheep who wandered away. But now you have turned to your Shepherd, the Guardian of your souls."

_____

_____

_____

_____

_____

_____

_____

_____

_____

_____

_____

_____

_____

210

Isaiah 40:31 (NIV) "but those who hope in the LORD will renew their strength. They will soar on wings like eagles; they will run and not grow weary, they will walk and not be faint." Psalm 23:3 (NKJV) "HE RESTORES MY SOUL."

Yes, Lord, I need this strength today. However, who or from what source am I relying on to receive it from? The Almighty, the Lifter of my head, the Beginning and the End, let us yield and surrender to Him today. The One True God. The lover of our souls!

_____

_____

_____

_____

_____

_____

_____

_____

_____

_____

_____

_____

_____

_____

211

"God, I feel judged by you. I continue to do too many wrong actions to receive Your love and approval. I am not worthy.", I said.

"Who told you that!?", God replied.

Who keeps telling us we are too far away, or too fallen, to receive God's amazing love and mercy?

Lamentations 3:22, 23 (NIV)

22 "Because of the Lord's great love we are not consumed, for his compassions never fail. 23 They are new every morning; great is your faithfulness."

"Give thanks to the God of heaven. His love endures forever" (Psalm 136:26).

1 John 4:19 (NIV)

"We love because he first loved us."

_____

_____

_____

_____

_____

_____

_____

_____

_____

_____

Easter, what's it all about?!

"...Why are you looking among the dead for someone who is alive? He isn't here! He is risen from the dead!" Luke 24:5,6 (NLT)

"We had hoped he was the messiah who had come to rescue Israel..." Luke 24:21

"...They said his body was missing, and they had seen Angels who told them Jesus is alive! Some of our men ran out to see, and sure enough, Jesus body was gone, just as the women had said."

Luke 24:23,24 (NLT)

"And he said, 'Yes, it was written long ago that the Messiah would suffer and die and rise again from the dead on the third day. It was also written that this message would be proclaimed in the authority of his name to all the nations, beginning in Jerusalem: There is forgiveness of sins for all who repent" ' " Luke 24:46,47 (NLT)

_____

_____

_____

_____

_____

_____

_____

_____

_____

213

Jesus opened the door to coming into the presence of God. If He opened it, and said, "Come!", then who are we to stay out? We are accountable to accept His work and offer. Today, let us not stay away for whatever reason. His sacrifice cleanses all. Let us enter in.

Understanding Easter, a bit more. Let's go deeper.

John 19:28-30 (NLT)

"Jesus knew that his mission was now finished, and to fulfill scripture he said, 'I am thirsty.' A jar of sour wine was sitting there, so they soaked a sponge in it, put it on a hyssop branch, and held it to his lips. When Jesus had tasted it, he said, 'It is finished!' Then he bowed his head and released his Spirit."

Below, are notes from the Life Application Study Bible on this verse.

"until this time, a complicated system of sacrifices had atoned for sins. Sin separates people from God, and only through the sacrifice of an animal, a substitute, could people be forgiven and become clean before God. But people sin continually, so frequent sacrifices were required, Jesus however, became the final and ultimate sacrifice for sin. The word "FINISHED" is the same as "PAID IN FULL". Jesus came to finish God's work of salvation, to pay the full penalty for our sins. With his death, the complex sacrificial system ended because Jesus took all sin upon himself. Now we can freely approach God because of what Jesus did for us. Those who believe in Jesus' death and Resurrection can live eternally with God and escape the penalty that comes from sin."

REJOICE! You may not hear people shout, "You're going to Hollywood!" But, worth infinitely more, we can now hear our God shout, "YOU'RE GOING TO HEAVEN!!!"

_____

_____

_____

214

When the DARKNESS is here, I will keep on RUNNING, for when the LIGHT COMES, I will have run FURTHER.

215

Happy Easter!

Luke 22:24-27 (NLT)

"Then they began to argue among themselves about who would be the greatest among them. Jesus told them, 'In this world the Kings and great men Lord it over their people, yet they are called friends of the people. But among you it will be different. Those who are the greatest among you should take the lowest rank, and the leader should be like a servant. Who is more important, the one who sits at the table or the one who serves? The one who sits at the table, of course, but not here! For I am among you as one who serves.'"

Rejoice you servants of the risen King of Kings!

_____

_____

_____

_____

_____

_____

_____

_____

_____

_____

_____

Philippians 2:5 (NLT)

"YOU MUST HAVE THE SAME ATTITUDE THAT CHRIST JESUS HAD."

What? @#! This changes my day quickly...reeling...how can I even begin?

If we seek, we will find. God can speak to us simply through His Word. Verse 3,4 "Don't be selfish; don't try to impress others. Be humble, thinking of others as better than yourselves. Don't look out only for your own interests, but take an interest in others too." This can change our day and relationships. Being a world changer can start with that which seems small. Peace. God is with us.

_____

_____

_____

_____

_____

_____

_____

_____

_____

_____

_____

_____

217

Now that Jesus has died and risen for the FORGIVENESS of our sins, what happens when we now sin again?

Hebrews 10:17,18 (NLT)

"Then he says, 'I will never again remember their sins and Lawless deeds.'

And when sins have been forgiven, there is NO NEED to OFFER any more sacrifices."

He came to set His children free.

_____

_____

_____

_____

_____

_____

_____

_____

_____

_____

_____

_____

_____

218

The FREEDOM from SIN and CONDEMNATION, we have it today!!

This is GLORIOUS! It makes me want to shout!!! ONE ACT, ONE PERSON, makes us free. It is a pass thrown to us by God, all we have to do is receive it.

Romans 5:15-18 (NLT) "But there is a great difference between Adam's sin and God's gracious GIFT. For the SIN of this one man, Adam, brought DEATH to many. But even greater is God's Wonderful GRACE and his gift of FORGIVENESS to many through this other man, JESUS CHRIST. And the result of God's gracious gift is very different from the result of that one man's sin. For Adam's sin led to CONDEMNATION, but God's FREE GIFT leads to our being MADE RIGHT with God, even though WE ARE guilty of many sins. For the sin of this one man, Adam, caused death to rule over many. But even greater is God's Wonderful GRACE and HIS gift of RIGHTEOUSNESS, for all who will RECEIVE IT will live in TRIUMPH over sin and death through this one man, JESUS CHRIST. Yes, Adam's one sin brings condemnation for everyone, but Christ's one act of righteousness brings a right RELATIONSHIP with God and a NEW LIFE for EVERYONE."

219

Let us remember where we are today. We are not in heaven yet. Our lives can now be filled with trials and heartbreaks, but let us stop and SMILE and remember whose we are and that we are only ON OUR WAY home. So, let us live with His power and joy today.

1 Peter 4:12,13 (NLT)

"Dear friends, don't be surprised at the fiery trials you are going through, as if something strange were happening to you. Instead, be very glad-- for these trials make you partners with Christ in his suffering, so that you will have the wonderful joy of seeing His glory when it is revealed to all the world."

God, is doing and will do, more in our lives than we could ever imagine! The last scripture before the book of Revelation deals with sin. When I am burdened with sin, I can be 'thankful' that it is, not just I, but God, who is able to keep us/me from falling away, and He, will bring us into His presence w/out a SINGLE FAULT. Without a single fault?! Only God could do this!

Jude 1:24,25 (NLT)

"Now all glory to God, who is able to keep you from falling away and WILL BRING YOU with great joy into his glorious presence without a single fault. All glory to Him who alone is God, our Savior through Jesus Christ Our Lord. All glory, majesty, power, and authority are His before all time, and in the present, and beyond all time! Amen."

In the Life Application Study Bible notes, it says, "To be sinless and perfect ("without a single fault") will be the ultimate condition of the believer when he or she finally sees Christ face to face. When Christ appears and we are given our new bodies, we will be like Christ. Coming into Christ's presence will be more wonderful than we could ever imagine!"

221

Some of Peter's last words on "The day of the Lord is coming."

2 Peter 3:11-13 (NLT)

"Since everything around us is going to be destroyed like this, what holy and godly lives you should live, looking forward to the day of God and hurrying it along. On that day, he will set the heavens on fire, and the elements will melt away in the flames. But we are looking forward to the new heavens and new earth he has promised, a world filled with God's righteousness."

Let us live TODAY for that which truly matters. JESUS. Let us thank Him for His GRACE! His grace opens the door for us to enter His kingdom and live how He wants us to live TODAY.

2 Peter 3:17,18 (NLT)

"You already know these things, dear friends. Be on guard so that you will not be carried away by the errors of these wicked people and lose your own secure footing. Rather, you must grow in the GRACE and knowledge of our Lord and Savior Jesus Christ. All glory to him, both now and forever! Amen."

_____

_____

_____

_____

_____

_____

_____

Being with Jesus is not only a one-time decision but is a daily coming into His presence, relationship, and allowing Him to change, even the way we think, now, today, every day. When we have access to His throne, why should we not come before Him daily. It is because our flesh is so easily influenced by the behavior and customs of this world that daily we need to be renewed. It is GRACE that we receive as a gift. It feels like I need this power to happen in my life every day. I need my heart and mind to be made right by Jesus' grace and power daily. The Holy Spirit in me will cleanse and renew my mind, IF I ALLOW Him!

Romans 12:1,2 (NLT) "And so, dear brothers and sisters, I plead with you to give your bodies to God because of all He has done for you. Let them be a living and holy sacrifice-- the kind He will find acceptable. This is truly the way to worship him. Don't copy the behavior and customs of this world, but LET God TRANSFORM you into a NEW PERSON by CHANGING the way you THINK. Then you will learn to know God's will for you, which is good and pleasing and perfect." Remember this is something He does in us, and for us. It is not by our own strength or efforts. We merely ALLOW Him to do what He is already offering us. A mind changing!

Are we struggling in life? God rested on the 7th day and He offers to us to enter into His REST now with Him.

Hebrews 4:7 (NLT) "So God set another time for entering his rest, and that time is TODAY."

Revelation 22:17 (NIV)

"The Spirit and the bride say, "COME!" And let the one who hears say, "Come!" Let the one who is thirsty come; and let the one who wishes take the FREE GIFT of the water of life." Do we really want to REST TODAY from the various struggles we are confronting? Do we really want the, "Water of Life" that is more satisfying than any drug or coffee?

This offer is so amazing, to enter His rest, to drink from the water of life, that He is calling all of us to take part in sharing with others this free amazing gift! We, who have received have been chosen to also say, "Come!", along with Him! Please remember...

This is a 'Limited Time Offer', and can only be redeemable through the King of Kings.

_____

_____

_____

_____

_____

_____

_____

_____

Find peace in Christ alone!

Sorry, troubles will come.

1 Thessalonians 3:2,3 (NLT)

"We sent him to strengthen you, to encourage you in your faith, and to keep you from being shaken by the troubles you were going through. But you know that we are DESTINED for such troubles." Let us find our peace alone, in Christ. If we are true followers of Christ, persecution is destined. He gives us a peace that passes our human understanding. PEACE

While we are still not yet 'perfected' in this life WE are STILL CALLED by God to SHINE. Do not carry false humility that only aids the enemies advance.

1 Corinthians 4:7 (NLT) "... What do you have that God hasn't given you? And if everything you have is from God, why boast as though it we're not a gift?"

What God gives must be given to others freely. We are not to judge ourselves or be judged by others as to whether or not we have the right to give it. It is a gift. Speak, share, give, love! It is not our own production! Do not remain silent!

NLT Study bible notes 4:7 "... failure to realize that everything is from God. There is no room for pride; humble gratitude is the only appropriate attitude."

_____

_____

_____

_____

_____

_____

_____

_____

_____

_____

_____

226

Things that really happened then, happen TODAY.

ACTS 16:18 (NLT) "This went on day after day until Paul got so exasperated that he turned and said to the demon within her, 'I command you in the name of Jesus Christ to come out of her.' and instantly it left her."

Have a nice day.

_____

_____

_____

_____

_____

_____

_____

_____

_____

_____

_____

_____

227

We are not called by God to do OUR work. We are called by God to do HIS work. When we look at it from the perspective of doing MY WORK given by God, we can easily get exhausted. It is always HIS work, from the beginning until the end. It is HIS WORK that we are called to do. When we do HIS work we also take part in HIS STRENGTH and REST. From the 'ministering' to the 'rest' let us have the perspective of doing His work. This suggests that we don't do His work alone. He is doing the work with us. We are just following what HE is doing. Although we are doing the ministering, IT IS HIS WORK! Catch this, and we will also catch His strength to do HIS WORK.

228

The LORD is WITH ME; I will not be afraid. What can MERE MORTALS do to me?

Psalm 118:6 (NIV)

What faith! Faith in God being with us; faith in God personally, actively, protecting us. No matter what we see, hear, or feel, we are good, because GOD is WITH US, on OUR SIDE, and by HIS DIVINE AUTHORITY and POWER, will act on our part and protect us THROUGH ALL THINGS. Peace TODAY.

Exodus 23:25 (NIV)

"Worship the LORD your God, and his blessing will be on your food and water. I will TAKE AWAY SICKNESS from among you,"

Correlation between worshiping God and health, humm...?

Well, what is true worship? Is it just singing or listening to songs? It can be a part of it, but it is so much more. "The highest form of praise and worship is OBEDIENCE to Him and His Word. To do this, we must know God."

Romans 12:1,2 (NLT)

"And so, dear brothers and sisters, I plead with you to give your bodies to God because of all he has done for you. Let them be a living and holy sacrifice—the kind he will find acceptable. THIS IS TRULY THE WAY TO WORSHIP HIM. 2 Don't copy the behavior and customs of this world, but let God transform you into a new person by changing the way you think. Then you will learn to know God's will for you, which is good and pleasing and perfect."

We can get to this point because of His mercies, because of who He IS, not ourselves alone, so let us not allow anything to stop us.

_____

_____

_____

_____

_____

_____

_____

When God chooses to ACT...! Let's keep our heads up high! AMAZING things are coming for God's children! The emphasis here is on "WHEN GOD CHOOSES TO ACT...", not on us, per say. Although we are called to partner with God, we are not equal partners. GOD does not have to do anything just because we speak it. He listens to and answers our prayers, but He acts at the time of His choice, with His, 'Will be done,' not our own.

Malachi 4:2,3 (NLT) "But for you who fear my name, the Sun of righteousness will rise with healing in his wings. And you will go free, leaping with joy like calves let out to pasture. On the day WHEN I ACT, you will tread upon the wicked as if they were dust under your feet, says the Lord Almighty."

There is something much, God's Kingdom, greater going on than what we see in front of us daily. The END is near. Keep our eyes on heaven, and let the trials refine us. Let's get focused now!

Daniel 12:1-4; 9,10 (NLT)

"At that time Michael, the archangel who stands guard over your nation, will arise. Then there will be a time of anguish greater than any since nations first came into existence. But at that time every one of your people whose name is written in the book will be rescued. Many of those whose bodies lie dead and buried will rise up, some to everlasting life and some to shame and everlasting contempt. Those who are wise will shine as bright as the sky, and those who turn many to righteousness will shine like stars forever. But you, Daniel, keep this prophecy a secret; seal up the book until the time of the end. Many will rush here and there and knowledge will increase."...

"But he said, 'Go now, Daniel, for what I have said is for the TIME OF THE END. Many will be purified, cleansed, and refined by these trials. But the wicked will continue in their wickedness, and none of them will understand. Only those who are wise will know what it means.'"

_____

_____

_____

_____

_____

_____

_____

_____

232

A few things...

When we feel our Lord Jesus using us powerfully we may start to feel the battle between self, or God, promotion. Are we trying to advance and glorify God or ourselves? Here was an attitude of Paul: Philippians 1:26 (NLT) "And when I come to you again, you will have even more reason to take PRIDE IN CHRIST JESUS because of what HE is doing THROUGH ME." HE IS DOING THROUGH ME! Let us not forget this as we boldly move forward as the Holy Spirit leads.

Our functioning, as we should, in our spiritual gifts, is for the GLORY of our Lord. When God chooses to ACT and He wants to use us, let us not tell Him we will 'pass' because we are not worthy! So, let's do this!

Secondly, I had this thought this morning, "We are like lighthouses." We are created to sit in this beautiful place. We go through storms, being slammed by enormous waves. Then, we have days of calm and peace when we look over God's created beauty, but, the pounding waves are guaranteed to return. They are only days away; like our trials in life. When we go through one, it says more are coming. But, they, WE, are CREATED FOR this purpose! We are made for this! In this position, they, we, are lights to the many who seek safe journey in this life.

_____

_____

_____

_____

_____

_____

_____

233

Let us not use religion for personal advancement. However, when God chooses to act through us, let us burn with all His fire we can. Yes, fire chases away the darkness and purifies that which remains.

Matthew 3:11 (NLT)

"I baptize with water those who repent of their sins and turn to God. But someone is coming soon who is greater than I am—so much greater that I'm not worthy even to be his slave and carry his sandals. He will baptize you with the Holy Spirit and with FIRE."

Lord Jesus, we ask that You IGNITE us today.

_____

_____

_____

_____

_____

_____

_____

_____

_____

_____

_____

_____

_____

234

Let us hear from God, the Word of God, and not be so quick to follow some leaders pop Christian new revelation bringing God down and man up. IF we want to be a part of, and move in God's power, when God moves, then we must not allow any ear tickling aberrations of God's word to set root, no matter what credentials, how charismatic or authoritative the teacher may seem.

Isaiah 46:8-13 (NLT)

"Do not forget this, you guilty ones, and do not forget the things I have done throughout history. For I am God--I alone! I am God, and there is no one else like me. Only I can tell you what is going to happen even before it happens. Everything I plan will come to pass, for I DO WHATEVER I WISH (God's truth-listen to it). I will call a swift bird of prey from the East--a leader from a distant land who will come and do my bidding. I have said I will do it, and I will. Listen to me, you stubborn, evil people! For I am ready to set things right, not in the distant future, but right now! I am ready to save Jerusalem and give my glory to Israel." This message was for a certain time in history for His children, but the lesson and word can be for us today too.

_____

_____

_____

_____

_____

_____

_____

ISAIAH 26:12 (NIV)

"LORD, you establish peace for us; all that WE have accomplished YOU have done FOR US."

YES, He does want us to accomplish, to succeed, to do great things. But, He wants us to humbly acknowledge His relationship, and presence, and love, in the fact that He is the One actually doing them FOR US; through us. I believe He also wants us to see that we are not just a tool he is using to be a blessing to others, but He is creating these accomplishments in our lives to be a blessing, FOR US, as well. Yes, God loves His children. He doesn't just USE us. He loves us, and does great things in our lives FOR US too.

There are many things God wants to do in our lives. One of the greatest, I believe, is that He SETS US FREE, soulfully and spiritually to SHINE for Him. We are created to shine. You are a LIGHT! Be a great LIGHT!

236

God's message for us on how to be, currently, in the craziness of the world we live in:

"SO BE TRULY GLAD." "What? Really!? How, God?", we might say back.

"Please listen my children..." He might say back to us, 1 Peter 1:3-7 (NLT) "All praise to God, the Father of our Lord Jesus Christ. It is by his great mercy that we have been born again, because God raised Jesus Christ from the dead. Now we live with GREAT EXPECTATION, and we have a PRICELESS INHERITANCE--an inheritance that is kept in heaven for you, pure and undefiled, BEYOND the REACH of change and decay. And through your faith, God IS PROTECTING YOU by his power until you receive this salvation, which is ready to be revealed on the last day for all to see. SO BE TRULY GLAD. There is WONDERFUL JOY ahead, even though you have to endure many trials for a little while. These trials will show that your faith is genuine. It is being tested as fire tests and purifies gold--though your faith is far more precious than mere gold. So when your faith remains strong through many trials, it will bring you much praise and glory and honor on the day when Jesus Christ is revealed to the whole world."

"OH!", God might add, "Did you hear me say that I am also at work personally PROTECTING YOU. No, I am not asleep! I am NOT in heaven with My hands tied, or bound until you pray to release them!

On your darkest day, when you were lost, and could not even lift your head or pray, I was there with you, protecting you from those who would destroy you!"

_____

_____

_____

_____

_____

Are we tired of the norm, just getting by? To turn that ship around and do anything great, or leave a legacy of greatness, we must live a life of sacrifices. Where will our chosen sacrifices be today? A life of comfort does not lead to greatness.

Romans 12:1 (BSB)

"Therefore, I urge you, brothers, on account of God's mercy, to offer your bodies as living sacrifices, holy and pleasing to God, which is your spiritual service of worship. Do not be conformed to this world, but be transformed by the renewing of your mind."

_____

_____

_____

_____

_____

_____

_____

_____

_____

_____

_____

_____

238

Acts 5:32 (NIV) "And we are witnesses of these things; and so is the Holy Spirit, whom God has given to those who OBEY Him."

I want to be careful to not share any wrong theology. Jesus sanctifies us by His sacrifice on the cross. It is His work; done, finished, complete. We are partners with God. Then, what is our part now in this sanctification, or is there a part we take? We are always, in His eyes, complete by the Blood of the Lamb and by His work alone. Our part now, is learning to use the tools He has given us to live in OBEDIENCE to Him. So, our part is to, through our free will, become obedient to the Holy Spirits leadings. We are called to lay our lives down as a living sacrifice. Do we wish to function more in FREEDOM and the POWER of the Holy Spirit? If so, then we must offer sacrifices of obedience to the Holy Spirits leading in our lives. No one said this Christianity was going to be easy. Thank Him for His mercy and grace. So... more obedience, more Holy Spirit; more Holy Spirit, more freedom and power, because He lives inside of us and even produces these desires within us. Glory to Jesus! More manifestations of the Holy Spirits working in our lives!

_____

_____

_____

_____

_____

_____

_____

_____

James 4:4-7 (NLT)

"You adulterers! Don't you realize that friendship with the world makes you an ENEMY of God? I say it again if you want to be a friend of the world, you make yourself an enemy of God. What do you think the scriptures mean when they say that the spirit God has placed within us is filled with envy? But he gives us even more grace to stand against such evil desires. As the scriptures say, 'God opposes the proud but favors the humble.' So, humble yourselves before God resist the devil, and he will FLEE FROM YOU. Come close to God and God will come close to you."

Church, you, me, He is talking to us!

_____

_____

_____

_____

_____

_____

_____

_____

_____

_____

_____

_____

_____

240

SEE THE NEWNESS.

Revelations 21:5 (NASB)

And He who sits on the throne said, "Behold, I am making ALL THINGS NEW."

Since You make all things new, help us to see with your eyes the newness, and the expectation of seeing the newness of all of your creation daily around us.

In our common everyday things, let's look for, and allow God to show us something new about these daily things, whatever they may be, people, etc., in our lives, today.

God sets us FREE from our enemies attacks so that we may experience His soul freeing love and then give it to others. Through all our running around in this place we call life, through all pursuits, highs and lows, we will be accountable, above all else, to this: Galatians 5:13 (NLT)"For you have been called to live in freedom, my brothers and sisters. But don't use your freedom to satisfy your sinful nature. Instead use your freedom to serve one another in love." Galatians 5:6 (NLT) "...What is important is Faith expressing itself in love."

To be able to GIVE, we must first RECEIVE. Let us open ourselves in prayer, and our hearts to receiving all God's amazing love for us today. With His love there is so much we can do.

This is AMAZING news! Better than any news we may find on any news station, or even winning the lottery!

Here it is:

1 Thessalonians 2:12 (NLT)"...For He called you to share in His KINGDOM and GLORY"

Do we really want this more than anything else? It is not that far away when all we have to do is ASK Him and RECEIVE.

_____

_____

_____

_____

_____

_____

_____

_____

_____

_____

_____

_____

_____

_____

Two days in a row I get scripture about God sharing His glory with His Children. Often times church goers may quote this scripture in Isaiah to prove He does not share His glory. This must be taken into context. Isaiah 42:8 "I am the LORD; that is my name. I will not give my glory to anyone else or the praise I deserve to idols." The GOOD NEWS: With His children, He does share His glory!

1 Thessalonians 2:12 (NLT) "...For He called you to share in His KINGDOM and GLORY"

2 Thessalonians 2:14 (NLT)"He called you to salvation when we told you the good news; now you can SHARE in the GLORY of our Lord Jesus Christ."

His presence and glory WITH US, changes ALL things. Praise Jesus Holy Name!

_____

_____

_____

_____

_____

_____

_____

_____

_____

_____

ARE WE MISSING SOMETHING HERE?!

2 COR 4:6 (NLT)

"For God, who said, "Let there be light in the darkness." has made this light shine in our hearts so we could know the glory of God that is seen in the face of Jesus Christ."

Our receiving everything, in the now, of what God has for us, is beyond our comprehension. Yet, it is there, to be poured out upon us, even more and more; His glory. To us who believe, ask, and receive, our lives may be changed in a flash.

_____

_____

_____

_____

_____

_____

_____

_____

_____

_____

_____

245

John 13:34 (BSB)

"A new commandment I give you: Love one another. AS I HAVE LOVED YOU, so you also must love one another."

No, the command is not to love others with whatever love, we already know, and have, it is to love

as He loves.

Honest truth, whatever love I have does not measure up to His love. How can I have God's love unless I know Him and become a changed person? Enter the Holy Spirit. Unless I GO SUPERNATURAL, into the Heavens, or, the heavens inside of me, I cannot love like Jesus. Unless I have a new Person, a new Spirit, THE HOLY SPIRIT, living inside of me, and taking control, I cannot love like Jesus! Unless we are BORN AGAIN (Jesus words. Not mine) from above, we cannot really LOVE at all. Because, GOD IS LOVE! We can have a form of human affection, but we cannot LOVE LIKE GOD, and this is exactly what we are called to do! We are called to have this divinity living INSIDE US. This is not controlled by man through some ritual. It comes like the wind, God controlled! 1 John 4:10 "This is real love-- not that we loved God, but that He loved us and sent His Son as a sacrifice to take away our sins."

Praise the Lord Jesus Christ, and let us ASK God to give us this otherworldly LOVE today.

_____

_____

_____

_____

_____

_____

246

Philippians 3:3 (NLT)

"For we who worship by the Spirit of God are the ones who are truly circumcised. We rely on what Christ Jesus has done for us. We put no confidence in human effort..."

So, He did it. Let us receive it. Be changed by it. Listen to it. Act on it. Watch it change our God given daily world. One by one.

_____

_____

_____

_____

_____

_____

_____

_____

_____

_____

_____

_____

_____

Hebrews 11:38-40 (NLT)

"They were too good for this world, wandering over deserts and mountains, hiding in caves and holes in the ground.

All these people earned a good reputation because of their faith, yet none of them received all that God had promised. For God had something better in mind for us, so that they would not reach perfection without us."

It is amazing to think that we are a part and linked to those great men and women of faith in the bible, and to think that we have something even greater in Jesus! If God chose us, and sees us this way, then how are we to be today? How are we to walk and have an effect in this world?

Hebrews 12:1,2 (NLT) says, "Therefore, since we are surrounded by such a huge crowd of witnesses to the life of faith, let us strip off every weight that slows us down, especially the sin that so easily trips us up. And let us run with endurance the race God has set before us. We do this by keeping our eyes on Jesus, the champion who INITIATES and PERFECTS our faith."

_____

_____

_____

_____

_____

_____

_____

_____

_____

_____

Anyone want spiritual gifts? Then ask the Holy Spirit. Anyone want community, relationships? The Holy Spirit gives us gifts to build one another up. This takes community. 1 Corinthians 12:11 (NLT) "It is the one and only Spirit who distributes all these gifts. He alone decides which gift each person should have."

LIFE APPLICATION STUDY BIBLE notes on this verse: "No matter what gift(s) a person has, all spiritual gifts are distributed by the Holy Spirit. The Holy Spirit decides which gifts each believer should have. We are responsible to use and sharpen our gifts, but we can take no credit for what God has freely given us."

_____

_____

_____

_____

_____

_____

_____

_____

_____

_____

_____

_____

Do we ever feel like, in our daily challenges and trials, maybe, kind of a bit, like King Asa in, 2 Chronicles 14:9-12 (NLT)

might have felt?

"Once an Ethiopian named Zerah attacked Judah with an army of 1,000,000 men and 300 chariots. They advanced to the town of Maresha, so Asa deployed his armies for battle in the valley north of Maresha. Then Asa cried out to the Lord his God, 'Oh Lord, no one but You can help the powerless against the mighty! Help us, O Lord our God, for we trust in You ALONE. It is in YOUR NAME that we have come against this vast horde. Oh Lord, You are our God; Do not let mere men Prevail against You!' So, the Lord defeated the Ethiopians in the presence of Asa and the army of Judah, and the enemy fled."

I pray Lord that with whatever battles we may face today, let us all rise up in prayer to You, and trust in You, GOD ALONE, to defeat our enemies!

I ask also that, each of us, may be able to hear God speak to us individually saying, "Remember, I love you!".

_____

_____

_____

_____

_____

_____

_____

_____

250

A true WAKE UP CALL for all of us. "We must stop grasping the temporary and begin focusing our time, money, and energy on the permanent: The Word of God and our eternal life in Christ."

Notes from Life Application Study Bible 1 Peter 1:24-25 (NLT)

Do we get tired of our bodies growing older, and the end of our lives growing closer? Chill!

1 Peter 1:23 (NLT)

"For you have been born again, but not to a life that will quickly end. Your new life will LAST FOREVER because it comes from the eternal, LIVING Word of God."

_____

_____

_____

_____

_____

_____

_____

_____

_____

_____

_____

_____

_____

_____

252

Turning back from our sinful ways is not just a sacrifice, giving something up, but It is a blessing to us. Good things on the way!

Acts 3:26 (NLT) "When God raised up his servant, Jesus, he sent Him first to you people of Israel, to BLESS YOU by turning each of you BACK from your sinful ways."

253

The WORD. Jesus is the Word. Read His words and take in the Breath of Life Himself. The Creator of all things. The One who can do all things. The Living Word, transferred from type to actually a person, the Holy Spirit living inside us. In 'Braveheart', the Mel Gibson character yelled out 'Freedom' from the oppression of a government. We now, can yell out 'Freedom!', from the oppression of even something much greater, death, satan and his hordes. Thank you, Jesus, for this victory!

254

Our fallen nature is already dead and we have been resurrected. We are now free, in Christ, from having to sin anymore. In coming to know Christ, the old nature controlled by sin has died. Yes, dead. So, we are free to produce a harvest of good deeds for God. Even though we may still allow our flesh to stumble us, it does not control us, only if we let it. We are born again and are now with His power. Being controlled by our sinful nature is dead. Gone! Bye bye!

Romans 7:6 (NLT)

"But now we have been released from the law. For we died to it and are no longer captive to its power. Now we can serve God. Not in the old way of obeying the letter of the law, but in the new way of living in the Spirit."

_____

_____

_____

_____

_____

_____

_____

_____

_____

_____

_____

If these were the end times. If Jesus return was only around the corner.

What would be one of God's most urgent messages to His people? Would it be,

Romans 6:12-14 (NLT), " Do not let sin CONTROL the WAY YOU LIVE, do not give in to sinful desires. Do not let any part of your body become an instrument of evil to SERVE sin. Instead, GIVE YOURSELVES COMPLETELY to God, for you were dead, but now you have NEW LIFE. So use your whole body as an instrument to do what is right for the glory of God. Sin is NO LONGER your master, for you no longer live under the requirements of the law. Instead you live under the FREEDOM of God's GRACE."

He is getting HIS CHILDREN READY.

256

Glory! "Why do we play football?", the coach asks all the players as they are sitting together in the gymnasium bleachers, for a meeting, at the beginning of the season. "Why do you play football?", the coach asks everyone. "Yes, you play it for the glory, the admiration from others, the women fawning over you, the comradery from teammates as they pat you on the back saying, 'Great job!', the newspaper articles with your name. You play it for the glory!

As we move on in our lives we can become players of a new team-"God's Kingdom"

In God's kingdom, and His earthly work and ministry, we now become part of this new team. We are still called to be a team member and even to do great things, as we function in the gifts of the Holy Spirit. When we do great things, in the flow of the gifts, it is only because the Holy Spirit gave it and did it. He gave us this supernatural ability. If I get a word of knowledge, if I pray for someone and they are physically healed, I did not do this. He used me. The results are totally Him. He gave it to me. When Daniel told the king what, exactly, the king had dreamed, it was because he was given this. He did not do this on his own. Glory to who? Our God! There will be a day when we share in His glory. When we see Him face to face and He says to us individually, "Well done, my good and faithful servant!" But today, let's be part of the game and minister God's love to others. Let's ask for, and allow, the Holy Spirit, to give us whatever gifts He chooses for us to have. Let us be bold in functioning in these gifts. He did it. He gave them. Now, the glory goes to Him. When, in the bible, the donkey spoke and warned the prophet, should they have praised the donkey for how wonderful he was for being able to speak a human language? Should they have written in the Jerusalem Times, "Amazing Self-Taught Donkey Speaks Aramaic." Of course not! God gives. We get. We act. God acts. Powerful, miraculous things happen. God did. God gets the glory. O' football player, this is not your day for individual glory. Let's go! Glorify the King!

The Word in agreement/confirmation/addition to yesterday's message.

God does the work. Glory to Jesus, not us.

Acts:3:12,13 (NLT)

Peter saw his opportunity and addressed the crowd. "People of Israel," he said, "What is so surprising about this? And why stare at us as though we had made this man walk by our own power or godliness? For it is the God of Abraham, Isaac, and Jacob-- the God of all our ancestors-- who has brought glory to his servant Jesus by doing this..." After being raised in the football life, one can still crave the glory given from others that was once attained. It can be a struggle. But we, and our spirit know, The glory belongs to Jesus! However, we are still called to make the plays and acts of love. They are His plays given to us by the Holy Spirit. Glory to Jesus! Let's go and finish our part of His game given to us!

258

Jonah 2:2 (NLT)

"I cried out to the Lord in my great trouble, and he answered me. I called to you from the land of the dead, and Lord, you heard me!"

Jonah 2:8 (NLT) "Those who worship false gods turn their backs on all God's mercies."

God is so bountiful with His grace and mercies offered to us. Turn to God today and receive them. He will rescue those who call upon His name.

_____

_____

_____

_____

_____

_____

_____

_____

_____

_____

_____

_____

_____

_____

Romans 11:17,18 (NLT)

"..., sharing in the rich nourishment from the root of God's special Olive tree. But you must not brag about being grafted in to replace the branches that were broken off. You are just a branch, not the root."

I wish to share in the rich nourishment from the root of God's special olive tree. I need it. The branch, us, does not feed the whole tree.

The branch, although beautiful in itself, exists to share the glory of the whole tree, and is fed by the root. Shine your beauty

and, remember, BE what you are a part of. He is with us TODAY.

_____

_____

_____

_____

_____

_____

_____

_____

_____

_____

_____

_____

260

To those who are God's children, the Word of God is a DELIGHT. Pick up God's Word and spend some time with IT. God is speaking to us. Start our days off with a DELIGHT!

Mark 12:37 (NLT)

"The large crowd listened to him with great Delight."

_____

_____

_____

_____

_____

_____

_____

_____

_____

_____

_____

_____

_____

_____

_____

How do we escape the worlds corruption caused by human desires? The worlds corruption is not just something outside of us that we see going on. It is inside of us too. Here in 2 Peter 1:1-4 (NLT) is what the Word of God says we need, "May God give you MORE and MORE GRACE and PEACE as you grow in your knowledge of God and Jesus our Lord. By HIS DIVINE POWER, God has given us everything we need for living a Godly life... and because of His glory and excellence, He has given us great and precious PROMISES. These are the promises that enable you to SHARE His DIVINE NATURE and escape the WORLD'S corruption caused by HUMAN DESIRES." I find it interesting that, if I am interpreting this correctly, as we grow in our knowledge of God and Jesus our Lord, the more and more GRACE we need. Sounds like the more we grow in knowledge of HIM the more we see our own fallen nature. Yet. He has given us the ability to SHARE in HIS DIVINE NATURE. His divine nature is corruption free.

262

If God wants us to walk and function in the supernatural power of Jesus, who are we to say 'no' to this? Jesus has called us to even do greater things than He did. Yup. The GLORY is part of the issue. It is not ours. It is His. This is what Peter said after his action of healing the lame beggars' legs.

Acts 3:12,13 (NLT)

"...'People of Israel,' he said, 'What is so surprising about this? And why stare at us as though we had made this man walk by our own power or godliness? For it is the God of Abraham, Isaac, and Jacob-- the God of all our ancestors-- who has brought GLORY to His servant JESUS by doing this....'"

ROMANS 2:16 (NLT)

"And this is the message I proclaim-- that the day is coming when God, through Christ Jesus, will judge everyone's secret life."

Mine too. Jesus have mercy. And, He does.

The world seems to be pretty attractive at times and everything within it, but the Holy Spirit stirs inside calling, "There is more! Listen and seek Me! I will be there!"

Galatians 5:25 (NLT) "Since we are living by the Spirit, let us follow the Spirit's leading in every part of our lives."

Gal 5:22,23 (NLT)

"But the Holy Spirit produces this kind of fruit in our lives: love, joy, peace, patience, kindness, goodness, faithfulness, gentleness, and self-control. There is no law against these things!"

The world may look attractive, but God offers so much more, along with fulfillment now and fulfillment for eternity!

_____

_____

_____

_____

_____

_____

_____

_____

_____

_____

When following this world and what it has to offer who are we really following?

We, as humans, except in Christ, are not immune to this evil commander of the powers in the unseen world. Some of us think we are free, but we really are not. Some of us have found true freedom in God's grace. As Bob Dylan said, "YOU GOTTA SERVE SOMEBODY."

Ephesians 2:1-5 (NLT)

"Once you were dead because of your disobedience and your many sins. You used to live in sin, just like the rest of the world, obeying the devil-- the commander of the powers in the unseen world. He is the spirit at work in the hearts of those who refuse to obey God. All of us used to live that way, following the passionate desires and inclinations of our sinful nature. By our very nature we were subject to God's anger, just like everyone else. But God is so rich in mercy, and he loved us so much, and even though we were dead because of our sins, he gave us life when he raised Christ from the dead. (It is only by God's grace that you have been saved!).

266

John 8:36 (NIV)

"So, if the SON sets you free, you will be free indeed."

It is done. It is finished. Everything we yearn for in this human life is accomplished for us in this one sentence.

BE FREE!!! Who knew? The philosophers like Plato, Socrates, Confucius, or Roman military might, the Jews fighting for freedom, the New World Order, all seeking their way. Who knew, that The Way would be so readily available today, even right now, by THE SON!!!

_____

_____

_____

_____

_____

_____

_____

_____

_____

_____

_____

While we live in a fallen world and this fall is gaining speed right before our eyes, how do I wish to live today? How do I wish to live in a world where the news wants to crush our hope daily. The world news presents chaotic situations, out of control, that call for their own political savior to come, not Jesus.

Romans 15:13 (NLT)

"I pray that God, the source of Hope, will fill you completely with joy and peace because you trust in Him. Then you will overflow with confident hope through the power of the Holy Spirit."

The world cannot offer this.

_____

_____

_____

_____

_____

_____

_____

_____

_____

_____

_____

_____

268

As we go through our daily journeys let us take a moment and think upon what is most important.

Galations 5:6 (NLT)

"...What is important is faith expressing itself in love."

Peace.

_____

_____

_____

_____

_____

_____

_____

_____

_____

_____

_____

_____

_____

_____

269

Who you TRULY ARE is not based upon anyone else's opinion, or, your own opinion. You are who God created you to be. Your emotions and thoughts do not change this reality. Rejoice in who God created you to be, finding new boldness and confidence in the awesomeness of the REAL YOU.

270

Happy 4th! We celebrate freedom and the founding of our country. No matter how great our country is, true freedom though is only to be found in the SPIRIT of the LORD JESUS.

2 Cor 3:17 (NLT)

"Now the Lord is the Spirit, and where the Spirit of the Lord is, there is freedom."

NO MATTER WHO WE ARE, WE CAN ONLY FIND TRUE FREEDOM IN THE SPIRIT OF THE LORD!

271

2 Cor 12:10 (NLT)

"...For when I am weak, then I am strong."

Dependence on God in ALL things! Rely upon HIS grace. He can and will take us to where we cannot go on our own.

_____

_____

_____

_____

_____

_____

_____

_____

_____

_____

_____

_____

_____

_____

Revelations 22:16 (NLT)

"... I am the bright morning star."

He is the "Light of Salvation" to all.

I am very glad, even though I am called to be one of many lights to this world, that I am not THEE LIGHT to this world. I fall so short to be THEE LIGHT to the world. And I don't think I can reach that far. Neither do I believe any of us humans can be THEE LIGHT to the world. I know Jesus said that we are now the light of the world. However, that being the case it did not dethrone Him from being THE ONE LIGHT source we all receive and take our light from. He still remains the One Morning Star, The Light of the World, the Light of Salvation. With that being said, let us get our light from THEE ONE LIGHT source and let it shine on those God puts in our paths today. He has a purpose for each of us. Life is short. Let us be empowered by, not our own strength, but by the Holy Spirit, who now lives within us, and who is now calling us to love 'AS JESUS LOVES' those He has put in our path. We cannot love 'as Jesus' loves unless we are supernaturally empowered. Whether you are in Peru or the U.S., God has opened up His door that we may enter, not by our own virtue, but by His mercy and grace. Let us not miss this opportunity, today, to be transformed by His LOVE and POWER this day and be poured out on those around us in need. Let HIS love shine in and through us. "The greatest of these IS LOVE." HOLY SPIRIT SHINE!

_____

_____

_____

_____

_____

I pick up the book. I see such beautiful WORDS of power and truth; mind shifting. I share...

1 John 2:7,8 (NLT)

"Dear friends, I am not writing a new commandment for you; rather it is an old one you have had from the very beginning. This old commandment-- to love one another-- is the same message you heard before. Yet it is ALSO NEW. Jesus lived the truth of this commandment, and YOU ALSO are living it. For the DARKNESS IS DISAPPEARING, and the True Light is already shining."

Let the darkness just FALL OFF of us today. Jesus is doing this. Let Him do his work IN US today.

_____

_____

_____

_____

_____

_____

_____

_____

_____

_____

_____

274

Brothers and sisters, cling onto God's will for your life. Remember that when we wake up, we don't just wake up to a physical world where random occurrences rule. Rather, we wake up to the unseen Kingdom of God, where His will ultimately rules. When we are children of God, there is power all around us. Things, good or bad, don't randomly rule in our lives. The law of entropy does not rule in our lives. Even what was meant for evil to happen to us, by man, or Satan, will not prevail.

Acts 26:14 (NLT)

'We all fell down, and I heard a voice saying to me in Aramaic, Saul, Saul, why are you persecuting me? It is useless for you to fight against my will.'"

Yes, to those called upon for His purpose, all happens for the good. To fight against God's purpose and will is useless. May God's will be victorious in our lives today.

_____

_____

_____

_____

_____

_____

_____

_____

_____

_____

_____

To receive the "Good News" of God's Word we must always see things through God's Kingdom eyes, not the world's. The Good News is that we come closer to Him. This is the summation.

Check out this Good News, 2 Tim 3:12 (NLT) "Yes, and everyone who wants to live a Godly life in Christ Jesus will suffer persecution." What!? Isn't the good news a huge bank account, an earthly mansion, comfort and pleasure? Didn't you suffer Lord, so that we wouldn't have too? 'Show me the money!' Is knowing God Himself our passion? Or, are things of this world our passion? Help us Father to see truth with Your pure eyes.

Don't we really want God's truth to be the opposite, than what it says, for ourselves and for others?

God's wake up call to all Christians:

Matthew 7:13,14 (NIV)

"Enter through the narrow gate. For wide is the gate and broad is the road that leads to destruction, and many enter through it. 14 But small is the gate and narrow the road that leads to life, and only a few find it."

_____

_____

_____

_____

_____

_____

_____

_____

_____

_____

_____

_____

_____

Can we ever finally become good enough to earn God's favor? The more I try, the further I seem to be.

Revelation 5:9 (NLT)

"...For you were slaughtered, and your BLOOD has RANSOMED PEOPLE for God from every tribe and language and people and nation. And YOU have CAUSED them to become a Kingdom of PRIESTS for our God. And they will REIGN on the earth." He has done it. Let's receive it.

_____

_____

_____

_____

_____

_____

_____

_____

_____

_____

_____

_____

_____

_____

Its my day off today. I have a list of what I need to do. What am I going to do? Ok, I am going to have PEACE in my relationship with God today. To find Christ, and, peace with God, we must simply believe in "the message that is close at hand."

There is nowhere to go to get this done. It is here, with us.

Romans 10:8-13 (NLT)

"...'The message is very close at hand; it is on your lips and in your heart.'

And that message is the very message about faith that we preach: if you confess with your mouth that Jesus is Lord and believe in your heart that God raised him from the dead, you will be saved. For it is by believing in your heart that you are made right with God, and it is by confessing with your mouth that you are saved. As the scriptures tell us, 'Anyone who trusts in Him will never be disgraced.' Jew and Gentile are the same in this respect. They have the same Lord, who gives generously to all who call on him. For everyone who calls on the name of the Lord will be saved."

We must see that there is no where we must go or something we must do. If we JUST CALL on Him, He is here to save us and bring peace. PEACE!

_____

_____

_____

_____

_____

_____

_____

Do we, you, me, have a ministry?

Yes, it is the ministry of Jesus. It is not, 'my ministry' or 'your ministry'. Jesus is the owner and producer. It is His ministry. We have the ministry of Jesus!

Mark 16:15-20 (NLT)

"And then He told them, go into all the world and preach the good news to everyone. Anyone who believes and is baptized will be saved. But anyone who refuses to believe will be condemned. These miraculous signs will accompany those who believe: they will cast out demons in My name, and they will speak in New languages. They will be able to handle snakes with safety, and if they drink anything poisonous, it won't hurt them. They will be able to place their hands on the sick, and they will be healed."

Yes, we have a ministry. It is Jesus', and it is glorious!

_____

_____

_____

_____

_____

_____

_____

_____

_____

_____

280

Do we only look for, or count upon our help being from man alone? It's wild! We have this mind blowing, divine, graced out, connection with God Almighty who wants to show up and do amazing things in our lives, but we live, and search for help, like it all relies upon ourselves or other people humans. Today, through prayer, let us ask Him, and trust Him to get involved in our personal lives and set us free.

Hebrews 13:5-6 (NIV)

5 "Keep your lives free from the love of money and be content with what you have, because God has said, "Never will I leave you; never will I forsake you." 6 So we say with confidence, "The Lord is my helper; I will not be afraid. What can mere mortals do to me."

281

Let us take a look at the CROSS again! It is the very POWER of God!

1 Corinthians 1:24,25 (NLT)

"But to those called by God to salvation, both Jews and gentiles, Christ is the power of God and the wisdom of God. This foolish plan of God is wiser than the wisest of human plans, and God's weakness is stronger than the greatest of human strength."

1 Corinthians 1:18,19 (NLT)

"The message of the CROSS is foolish to those who are headed for Destruction! But we who are being saved know it is the VERY POWER OF GOD. As the scriptures say,

'I will destroy the wisdom of the wise and discard the intelligence of the intelligent.'

On this mountain... On this mountain! Through trust in Him, look what God does in our lives. As we live our lives, let us cling to trusting our Lord and expect His greatness to show up!

ISAIAH 25:6-9 (NIV)

6 On this mountain the LORD Almighty will prepare a feast of rich food for all peoples, a banquet of aged wine— the best of meats and the finest of wines.

7 On this mountain He will destroy the shroud that enfolds all peoples, the sheet that covers all nations;

8 He will swallow up death forever. The Sovereign LORD will wipe away the tears from all faces; he will remove his people's disgrace from all the earth. The LORD has spoken.

9 In that day they will say, "Surely this is our God; we trusted in Him, and He saved us. This is the LORD, we trusted in Him; let us rejoice and be glad in His salvation."

_____

_____

_____

_____

_____

_____

_____

_____

283

After all the doing, the victories, the defeats, the efforts, the achievements, the battles, the grind, the failures, the stumbling and falling, I just need to know this: God LOVES me.

Romans 8:38,39 (NIV)

38 For I am convinced that neither death nor life, neither angels nor demons, neither the present nor the future, nor any powers, 39 neither height nor depth, nor anything else in all creation, will be able to separate us from the love of God that is in Christ Jesus our Lord."

God is with us. He is so close to us. He already knows what we are thinking before we speak. Sometimes, He even gave us those thoughts in our pursuit for Him, and His pursuit for us. He is there with His hand held out to us, ready to act. We only need to ASK.

Psalm 30:2 (NIV)

2 "LORD my God, I called to you for help, and you healed me."

_____

_____

_____

_____

_____

_____

_____

_____

_____

_____

_____

_____

_____

285

I want newness born into my life, but not by HUMAN EFFORT, but buy the POWER OF THE SPIRIT!

Galatians 4:29 (NLT)

"But you are now being persecuted by those who want you to keep the law, just as Ishmael, the child born by HUMAN EFFORT, persecuted Isaac, the child born by the POWER of the SPIRIT."

_____

_____

_____

_____

_____

_____

_____

_____

_____

_____

_____

_____

_____

_____

_____

286

Be still today and know that Jesus:

Colossians 1:15-20 (NLT)

"... existed before anything was created and is supreme over all creation...

Made the things we can see and the things we can't see-- such as thrones, kingdoms, rulers, and authorities in the unseen world.

Everything was created through Him and for Him. He existed before anything else and He holds all creation together.... through him God reconciled everything to

Himself. He made peace with everything in heaven and on earth by means of Christ's Blood on the cross."

BE STILL AND KNOW THIS.

_____

_____

_____

_____

_____

_____

_____

_____

_____

God is not waiting for us to change ourselves, He is waiting for us to ALLOW Him to make the changes in our life that He already wants to make. It is about His desire and power to change us, not our own. What does God desire to be manifested in our lives? "The HEART of the matter: TOTAL TRANSFORMATION."

Romans 12:1,2 (NLT)

"And so, dear brothers and sisters, I plead with you to give your bodies to God because of all He has done for you. Let them be a living and holy sacrifice-- the kind He will find acceptable. This is truly the way to worship him. Don't copy the behavior and customs of this world, but LET God TRANSFORM you into a NEW person by CHANGING the way you THINK. Then you will learn to know God's will for you, which is good and pleasing and perfect."

_____

_____

_____

_____

_____

_____

_____

_____

_____

_____

_____

288

NOTHING GREATER!!!

1 THESS 5:9 (NLT)

"For God chose to SAVE US through our lord Jesus Christ, NOT TO pour out His ANGER on us."

God deserves our thanks and praise today!

_____

_____

_____

_____

_____

_____

_____

_____

_____

_____

_____

_____

Here is a serious wake up call to not so easily live with sin in our lives.

Genesis 4:7 "If you do what is right, will you not be accepted? But if you do not do what is right, sin is crouching at your door; it desires to have you, but you must rule over it."

But, now, here is the great GOOD NEWS! We do not do this alone! Our Almighty loving heavenly Father is with us, inside us, making this holiness happen! We are not alone in this process.

1 THESS 5:23,24 (NLT)

"Now may the God of peace make you holy in every way, and may your whole spirit and soul and body be kept blameless until our Lord Jesus Christ comes again. GOD WILL MAKE THIS HAPPEN, for he who calls you is faithful."

Peace. We are in God's hands.

_____

_____

_____

_____

_____

_____

_____

_____

_____

290

"What is God's WILL for my life?" Do we ever struggle with this question? Here it is. It is internal not external.

1Thess 5:16,17,18 (NLT)

"ALWAYS be JOYFUL. NEVER stop PRAYING. Be THANKFUL in ALL circumstances, for this is GOD'S WILL for YOU who BELONG to CHRIST JESUS."

_____

_____

_____

_____

_____

_____

_____

_____

_____

_____

_____

_____

_____

What does Jesus want for us today as we walk and live on His planet? He wants the PEACE that He gives us to reign in our hearts. Do we have His peace today? And, He calls us to walk out the holiness He gave us. He wants us to not just, 'not do' certain things, but to be focused on 'doing' certain things. We are called to 'live out' a wonderful life, and not just be 'not doers'.

Colossians 3:12-15 (NLT)

"Since God chose you to be the holy people He loves, you must clothe yourselves with tenderhearted mercy, kindness, humility, gentleness, and patience. Make allowance for each other's faults, and forgive anyone who offends you. Remember, the Lord forgave you, so you must forgive others. Above all, clothe yourselves with love, which binds us all together in perfect harmony. And let the peace that comes from Christ rule in your hearts. For as members of one body you are called to live in peace. And always be thankful."

Aren't we all addicts in one form or another? We are addicted to sin. Worse maybe, we're not just addicted, but sin is actually in our very nature. It is my nature, and I can't just give it up no matter how hard I try. A dog cannot give up being a dog. I cannot change my own nature. I must receive a new nature. I must be born again. I must be created anew. This is what He did for me! And, if I allow Him to, He can even change the way I think. I cannot do this in my own strength. Neither can I please God by exercising my own strength and power. He must do it. I please God by receiving what He has done for me. Enter the Lord Jesus. He took on the death penalty of these sinful natures of ours and died in our place. Now, by Him, in Him, through Him, we have been freed. He has now given us a new Holy nature; the Holy Spirit, who now lives inside those who ask for Him. It is now by our trust, faith. If I try to be a new, sin free person, by not sinning, through following the law, I end up back facing my sinful self once again. But, when I trust in His offering for me, I am free and holy.

Galatians 3:11,12 (NLT)

"So, it is clear that no one can be made right with God by trying to keep the law. For the Scriptures say, 'It is through faith that a righteous person has life.' This way of faith is very different from the way of law, which says, 'It is through obeying the law that a person has life.'

But Christ has rescued us from the curse pronounced by the law. When he was hung on the cross, he took upon Himself the curse for our wrongdoing. For it is written in the scriptures, 'cursed is everyone who is hung on a tree.' Through Christ Jesus, God has blessed the Gentiles with the same blessing he promised to Abraham, so that we who are believers might receive the promised Holy Spirit through faith."

So, to those of us who may be burdened by the 'Addiction to sin', let us look no further than the Cross of Christ, ask for forgiveness, and receive the abundant life and transformation of a new holy nature, God's love within us, the Holy Spirit. He loves us.

293

Good news today!

God just doesn't give up on us.

Lamentations 3:31-32 (NIV)

"31 For no one is cast off by the Lord forever. 32 Though he brings grief, he will show compassion, so great is his unfailing love."

_____

_____

_____

_____

_____

_____

_____

_____

_____

_____

_____

_____

_____

_____

_____

294

What is our daily hope?

Acts 4:2 (NLT)

"These leaders were very disturbed that Peter and John were teaching the people that through Jesus there is a resurrection of the dead."

For all of us, the bodies we are in right now are not the end. We will be RESURRECTED 'THROUGH JESUS!' Although we cannot see it now, we will experience this.

_____

_____

_____

_____

_____

_____

_____

_____

_____

_____

_____

_____

295

We can rejoice and FIND JOY in God our Savior, no matter our physical or material position. That's how great our God is!

Habakkuk 3:17-18 (NIV)

"Though the fig tree does not bud and there are no grapes on the vines, though the olive crop fails and the fields produce no food, though there are no sheep in the pen and no cattle in the stalls, yet I will rejoice in the LORD, I will be joyful in God my Savior."

God doesn't tell us not to sin just so that we won't do something. He tells us not to sin and tells us to repent of sinning because He wants to bless us. He wants to give us times of refreshment. He wants to give us His presence. And when we turn from our sins he is offering us blessings, refreshment and His presence, not just a barren dry desert.

Acts 3:19,20 (NLT)

"Now repent of your sins and turn to God, so that your sins may be wiped away. Then times of refreshment will come from the presence of the Lord..."

Acts 3:26 (NLT)

"...to bless you by turning each of you back from your sinful ways."

Who are we? Salesperson, mother, daughter, son, father, manager, firefighter, teacher, athlete, homeless, failure, world leader? We hear our identity pounding in our minds, our souls. We hold on, fight off, reaching for or trying to let go of these rungs as we climb on this ladder of life.

But, Jesus comes to us today in the midst of our climb and says, "Peace and grace I give to you. THIS, is who you are:"

Galatians 4:4-7 (NLT)

"But when the right time came, God sent His Son, born of a woman, subject to the law. God sent Him to BUY FREEDOM for us who were slaves to the law, so that he could adopt us as his very own children. And because we are HIS CHILDREN, God has sent the Spirit of his Son into our hearts, prompting us to call out, 'Abba Father.' Now you are no longer a slave but God's own child. And since you are his child, God has made you his heir."

"THIS IS WHO YOU ARE!"

_____

_____

_____

_____

_____

_____

_____

_____

What???!!! Do we want true UNITY without discrimination? Then wake up you supposedly 'woke' people and put on Christ. This is where there is true unity. It's not even about sexual gender. Male and female are united in Christ. But wait, there is even more...

Galatians 3:24-29 (NLT)

"Let me put it another way. The law was our Guardian until Christ came; it protected us until we could be made right with God through faith. And now that the way of faith has come, we no longer need the law as our guardian.

For you are all children of God through faith in Christ Jesus. And all who have been United with Christ in baptism have PUT ON CHRIST, LIKE PUTTING ON NEW CLOTHES. There is no longer Jew or Gentile, slave or free, male and female. For you are all one in Christ Jesus. And now that you belong to Christ, you are the true children of Abraham. You are his heirs, and God's promise to Abraham belongs to you."

God's promise to Abraham belongs to you! Think about this. Here is God's promise to Abraham. Genesis 12:1-3 (NIV)

"Go from your country, your people and your father's household to the land I will show you.

"I will make you into a great nation, and I will bless you;

I will make your name great, and you will be a blessing.

I will bless those who bless you, and whoever curses you I will curse;

and all peoples on earth will be blessed through you."

Are we READY to allow the Holy Spirit to change, even the way we think???

_____

_____

_____

_____

299

Isn't it beautiful to hear truth! We recognize that we are prisoners of sin, but God shows us the way to break out! Believe in Jesus! With that belief, let us spend time with Him today and allow Him to change us with His Word and presence.

Galatians 3:22 (NLT)

"But the scriptures declare that we are all prisoners of sin, so we receive God's promise of freedom only by believing in Jesus Christ."

300

PHILIPPIANS 1:21 (NLT)

"For to me, living means living for Christ, and dying is even better."

Such a high calling.

Convicted in my soul, but not condemned. I hear the call. He's calling us deeper, HIGHER.

_____

_____

_____

_____

_____

_____

_____

_____

_____

_____

_____

_____

_____

301

Where is the sanity? Where is the true rest? Where is our hope and peace within the craziness of our current world?

Psalm 46:10 (NLT)

"Be still and know that I am God! I will be honored by every nation. I will be honored throughout the world."

_____

_____

_____

_____

_____

_____

_____

_____

_____

_____

_____

_____

_____

_____

302

Satan, I believe, wants us so caught up with worries, anxieties, unjust afflictions, and the pleasures of this world, that we STOP praising and worshiping God! If he can get our eyes off the Almighty lover of our souls, and stop us from praising and worshiping Him his goal is achieved. But God still stands for us and with us. He is faithful to His children even when we forget or do not recognize His goodness to us.

Psalm 48:1-10

"How great is the Lord, how deserving of praise, ... O God, we meditate on your unfailing love as we worship in your Temple. As your name deserves, O God, you will be praised to the ends of the earth. Your strong right hand is filled with victory."

Rebellion against God. To be "in the flesh", Paul uses this term "negatively to denote human existence apart from God. To be 'in the flesh' is to be dominated by sin and its HOSTILITY to God" "When we are in REBELLION against God, his commands spark in us a desire to do the exact opposite of what he commands." Makes me think anew the gravity of what my sin means. It means much more than just doing something I may get a little pleasure over, or a feeling of control over. My sin is rebellion against, and hostility towards God. Eye opening.

Romans 7:4

"So, my dear brothers and sisters, this is the point: you died to the power of the law when you died with Christ. And now you are united with the One who was raised from the dead. As a result, we can produce a harvest of Good Deeds for God."

Quotations are from NLT Study Bible notes on Romans 7.

304

With the world in all its craziness, I see Jesus standing before us and saying to us, as he did to Mary when she was at the tomb looking for Him, "Dear woman, why are you crying?"

I believe He is saying the same to us today as He stands before us. "Dear child of mine, no matter how dismal things may appear, it is I, Jesus. I am alive and I am with you. Do not fear. Certain things must happen, but I will never leave you. I will never forsake you. Take my hand child."

305

Please stop being ALONE out there!

Acts 9:31 (NLT) "The church then had peace throughout Judea, Galilee, and Samaria, and it became stronger as the Believers lived in the fear of the lord. And with encouragement of the Holy Spirit, and also grew in numbers."

Christian brothers and sisters we are called to live in COMMUNITY. In this community, we are called to live together in the FEAR OF the LORD. And with the ENCOURAGEMENT of the Holy Spirit. Fear of God and encouragement; two things we cannot live life to the full without. God is Holy.

We need the presence of the Holy Spirit who comforts us and lets us know that 'yes' we are God's children and that He is with us. The Holy Spirit then, if we allow Him, changes us and makes us holy. The Holy Spirit gives us the power to know that His presence overcomes all things. He's all we need and everything that we need.

The Word says that LOVE overcomes a multiple of sins. Jesus said that we must love others AS HE LOVES others. So let us see that we are called to not just love others with our own love, but rather with a supernatural love, born of God. This is why we need the God, make me new, divine, Holy Spirit connection. And we can have this, and be changed by heaven today if we simply ask. God's Kingdom and power is waiting.

_____

_____

_____

_____

_____

We really need to live by, "THE POWER OF HIS NAME". Not only should we believe in Him, but we are also called to do great things. Why? Because He said so. By His name His power resides in us. Let's use it.

John 20:30,31 (NLT)

"The disciples saw Jesus do many other miraculous signs in addition to the ones recorded in the book. But these are written so that you may continue to believe that Jesus is the Messiah, the son of God, and that by believing in him you will have life by the power of His name."

_____

_____

_____

_____

_____

_____

_____

_____

_____

_____

_____

_____

_____

307

The joy of being forgiven. Jesus went through death to set us free from sin. Now we can be. Peace. Don't give up. Continue to grow and return to the Lord. We don't have to keep on sinning any longer. Even when we stumble, we are still free! Because He has bought our freedom by His blood and death upon the cross. Yes, He did it for us each, individually, when He died on the cross.

1 John 5:18,19 (NLT)

"We know that God's children do not make a practice of sinning, for God's Son holds them securely, and the evil one cannot touch them. We know that we are children of God and that the world around us is under the control of the evil one."

The world around us is under the control of the evil one. We are not. We are free.

308

So, we are all sinners and have fallen short of the glory of God. All of us, no matter what position we may hold upon this earth. We are equally fallen. But we now, for us Christians, also live under His new covenant He has given us. Jeremiah 31:34 (NLT) "... And I will forgive their wickedness, and I will never again remember their sins."

Be free God's children.

Let us not get so caught up in the grind bummer of having to go to work. In the Bible, the word "worship" in Psalm 2:11 is the Hebrew word "abad" and it means, "to labor, work, do work and serve.". So, with our 'work' we are actually worshiping God.

So, we can go to a big concert for a time of worship and/or we can go to work. Praise Jesus in all things.

310

Our enemy, Satan, deceitfully tries to work his way into our lives, and minds, to take away our LOVE FOR OTHERS. God's word says, 'Those who are forgiven much, love much'. We are FREE because we ARE FORGIVEN, and because we are forgiven we LOVE others. Faith, is what saves us, and faith expresses itself through love of God and others. So, we can use our LOVE OF OTHERS as a monitor of faith. Is our love of others being crushed? Do we feel judgement, criticalness, offense, bitterness, resentment, sneaking into our relationships, choking out the flow of God's love? This is one thing our enemy slyly and covertly does to extinguish our God connected flames. I was on a walk around the neighborhood the other day and I was having a difficult time, mentally and emotionally, getting my mind off an egregious situation that had occurred a while back by a person in the neighborhood. As I was walking, stewing in the mental frustration, I walked by a young child and his mother who were working in their front yard. The young child called out, 'Hi!', 'Hi', I responded. He added, 'how are you doing?' 'Good!', I said, "How are you?" He responded with a "Good.", and he added after a hesitation, "Nice to meet you!" (I think his mom was training him). Amazing! The devil was insidiously trying to bring division against others, and division within myself, in effect, turning off the flow of love and caring to others, and then it was profoundly reeled back in by a child. This is what it is about. The channel of love, and caring for, and kindness, towards others seen in an act by a child brought me back to truth. I am here, not for vengeance, or to become, by offense, distant from others. But rather, I found the SWEETNESS of engaging in, and caring for others in the action of a child.

Truly I tell you," He said, Matthew 18:3 (NIV) "Unless you change and become like little children, you will never enter the kingdom of heaven."

____

____

Word to live by. Not just when life becomes difficult but also in taking on new challenges that bring growth and maturity to our lives and faith. Let's take those led challenges and let us dive in over our heads where we will meet the Holy Spirit.

Matthew 6:26,27 (NIV)

"Look at the birds of the air; they do not sow or reap or store away in barns, and yet your heavenly Father feeds them. Are you not much more valuable than they? Can any one of you by worrying add a single hour to your life?"

Go ahead. Make the dive. Sometimes its about waiting and allowing God to provide. Other times, its about taking the plunge and trusting God will provide.

_____

_____

_____

_____

_____

_____

_____

_____

_____

_____

_____

312

So important in the body of Christ, the church. The enemy tries to get within the church and create OFFENSE. There seems like there could even be a strong SPIRIT of OFFENSE slithering within and hovering over the body. God's Word and Spirit comes even stronger against this and shows how we must break this? We must do the opposite of feeling offense and becoming critical. These are Gods simple but powerful words:

1 Thess. 5:11 (NLT) "So encourage each other and build each other up, just as you are already doing."

My wife shared words to me, I believe that came from the Holy Spirit, that

when we feel this strong spirit of offense present we must literally force ourselves to go do the opposite within the body. We must not hesitate, but rather start, RIGHT NOW, go genuinely bless and ENCOURAGE SOMEBODY! The evil spirit will flee! Remember, the enemy wants also to get ahold of the way we think. He does not want us to have the mental freedom to be able to follow the Lord's command to, "Love one another as I have loved you."

_____

_____

_____

_____

_____

_____

_____

_____

313

Psalm 127:1 (NIV)

"Unless the LORD builds the house, the builders labor in vain. Unless the LORD watches over the city, the guards stand watch in vain."

We can rejoice today that the Lord is with us. He will accomplish, with us, far more than we ever could on our own. He is the 'LIFTER OF OUR HEADS'. If we allow Him to build the house, we don't strive, we REJOICE.

_____

_____

_____

_____

_____

_____

_____

_____

_____

_____

_____

_____

_____

'Just the facts Ma'am...'

1 Peter 1:6,7 (NLT)

"So be truly GLAD. There is WONDERFUL JOY ahead, even though you have to endure many trials for a little while. These trials will show that your FAITH is GENUINE. It is being tested as fire tests and PURIFIES gold--though YOUR FAITH is far more precious than mere gold. So when your faith remains STRONG through many trials, it will BRING YOU much PRAISE and GLORY and HONOR on the day when JESUS CHRIST is REVEALED to the WHOLE WORLD."

_____

_____

_____

_____

_____

_____

_____

_____

_____

_____

_____

_____

Can we really try today to do this? How deep and eternal the meaning of this FACT. How can this scripture have an impact on us today?

Psalm 46:10 (NIV)

"...Be still, and know that I am God; I will be exalted among the nations, I will be exalted in the earth."

_____

_____

_____

_____

_____

_____

_____

_____

_____

_____

_____

_____

_____

_____

_____

316

Looking at Revelations. So much heavenly majesty and action. I think about being there. I want to take part. Then I think that I do have a part, we do have a part. We were created to be a part of doing God's will, on earth as it is in heaven, today. Let Your mercy and grace be with us today, and let us be a part of Your heavenly actions today here on earth. Come Holy Spirit!

_____

_____

_____

_____

_____

_____

_____

_____

_____

_____

_____

_____

_____

We walk into church as human beings. But, we are so much more. At times, we carry our hurts, our jealousies, offenses, and more in with us. So we are mentally, emotionally, crippled in our worship and in loving one another as His command states, "A new command I give to you: You must love one another as I love you." The only way I know how to do that is by being transformed by Jesus, the Holy Spirit, actually changing the way I think. He must be inside me, actually making me a new person. To love as He loves; I must become a new person. Along with this call is a plea from the Lord to actually CHANGE our actions in church towards one another. This is so important that God is commanding us to go and do this now: CHANGE! Change by, 1 Thessalonians 5:11 (NLT), " So encourage each other and build each other up, just as you are already doing."

Let us go and look for ways to encourage one another. It might be a smile and hand shake as you look them in the eyes, or other means like praying for one another. It might be a hug, or? These actions can literally break the darkness!

I pray that each of us today would be individually BLESSED so that, we too, may be a blessing to others.

Shalom.

318

KNOW WHO YOU ARE.

New Living Translation

Galatians 3:9 (NLT)

"So, all who put their faith in Christ share the same blessing Abraham received because of his faith."

WHAT is Abrahams BLESSING?

"I will make you a great nation; I will bless you and make your name great; and you shall be a blessing.

I will bless those who bless you, and I will curse him who curses you; and in you all the families of the earth shall be blessed."' Genesis 12:2-3 (NKJV)

_____

_____

_____

_____

_____

_____

_____

_____

_____

_____

Elohim is a name for God in the bible. Meaning infinite-all powerful. They also shorten it to El then put another name describing Him. Like "El Roi" which means "The God who sees." Know that God sees everything we are going through. He is faithful to His children. He is with us. He loves us and has given us many promises. One is that HE, not us, or anyone else, WILL WORK ALL THINGS out for OUR good. What is that? God is the one who knows and is already in action working it out for us. So, we can be STILL and KNOW that God sees us, and has already put into play His plan for us. Though it may not be manifest yet to us here on earth, in Heaven, it is already done. Peace

320

Yes, I don't understand it. It is beyond me. But, we can rely on it. It is a miracle that happens when we cling to HIM.

Philippians 4:7 (NIV) "And the peace of God, which transcends all understanding, will guard your hearts and your minds in Christ Jesus."

PEACE

_____

_____

_____

_____

_____

_____

_____

_____

_____

_____

_____

_____

_____

'I Am your Father. You don't control anything. Know that I Am with you, controlling all things. Lay it down.'

_____

_____

_____

_____

_____

_____

_____

_____

_____

_____

_____

_____

_____

_____

_____

_____

322

What if every Sunday we had to come before the Almighty and be judged on whether or not we could enter into His presence, based upon what we did, or didn't do for that week? Did we earn His favor based upon our actions? Did we follow the law?

I am so thankful that this is not the Heavenly Father we know and follow. I am not worthy to enter, but when I am convicted and confess my sins, my Heavenly Father holds out His hand and says, "Come!"

We think of a humans last words as being so very important. God still continues to speak today, but as far as the Bible, God's written Word, His last words are so beautiful.

Revelation 22:21 (NLT)

"May the grace of the Lord Jesus be with God's holy people."

I pray we may, not hold back, but run into the presence of our loving Heavenly Father, and by His grace, receive all that we need and more. Peace.

_____

323

I come to God's Word daily. It is the place which wages WAR against the thoughts that lead us away from His strength and peace. In God's, beyond amazing, Word, we will find His presence. We will find security, shelter, and a sound mind. We may not realize it but there is a war going on for our minds. And, in the Bible, we find a living Word, a Holy Spirit alive Word. It will CHANGE us.

"We are human, but we don't wage war as humans do. We use God's Mighty weapons, not worldly weapons, to knock down the strongholds of human reasoning and to destroy false arguments. We destroy every proud obstacle that keeps people from knowing God. We capture their rebellious thoughts and teach them to obey Christ." 2 Cor 10:3-5 (NLT).

Romans 7:6 (NLT) "... now we can serve God, not in the old way of obeying the letter of the law, but in the new way of LIVING IN THE SPIRIT."

We need the Holy Spirit in us to obey and please God. It is not about obeying the letter of the law to get God's approval. It is about ALLOWING the HOLY SPIRIT to CHANGE us, even the way we think. JESUS, have grace upon us all and send us your Holy Spirit today that we may, live for You, and please You TODAY.

_____

_____

_____

_____

_____

_____

_____

_____

_____

_____

_____

_____

325

God LOVED the JAILER too!

Acts 16:23-32 (NLT)

They were severely beaten, and then they were thrown into prison. The jailer was ordered to make sure they didn't escape. So the jailer put them into the inner dungeon and clamped their feet in the stocks.

Around midnight Paul and Silas were praying and singing hymns to God, and the other prisoners were listening. Suddenly, there was a massive earthquake, and the prison was shaken to its foundations. All the doors immediately flew open, and the chains of every prisoner fell off! The jailer woke up to see the prison doors wide open. He assumed the prisoners had escaped, so he drew his sword to kill himself. But Paul shouted to him, "Stop! Don't kill yourself! We are all here!"

The jailer called for lights and ran to the dungeon and fell down trembling before Paul and Silas. Then he brought them out and asked, "Sirs, what must I do to be saved?"

They replied, "Believe in the Lord Jesus and you will be saved, along with everyone in your household." And they shared the word of the Lord with him and with all who lived in his household.

That day the jailer received God's GRACE. It is offered to us daily as well. Will we grasp it and receive it within us now, and also take it with us wherever we go? It is offered to us for FREE. Jesus already paid for it. Grace, grace, GRACE! It is yours.

_____

_____

_____

_____

_____

326

DON'T GIVE UP!!! DON'T GIVE UP!!!

There is Holy Spirit fire on the other side; a renewed mind with freedom, peace and power. The devil is rabid about us not seeing what is on the other side! We are God's powerful children. He is with us! Feel and see what is coming! DON'T GIVE UP!!!

1 Peter 4:12,13 (NLT)

"Dear friends, don't be surprised at the fiery trials you are going through, as if something strange were happening to you. Instead be very glad--for these trials make you partners with Christ in his suffering, so that you will have the wonderful joy of seeing his glory when it is revealed to all the world."

_____

_____

_____

_____

_____

_____

_____

_____

_____

_____

_____

Acts 11:18 (NLT) "When the others heard this, they stopped objecting and began praising God. They said, 'We can see that God has also given the Gentiles the PRIVILEGE of REPENTING of their sins and receiving eternal life.' "

The PRIVILEGE! God has given us the privilege of REPENTING of our sins and receiving ETERNAL LIFE. Repenting of our sins is such a great gift that opens the door to God's power and freedom in our lives. Having a 'privilege' is always a good thing. Repenting of one's sins is not a chore that we have to do, but rather a privilege. The American Heritage dictionary defines privilege:

"Such an advantage, immunity, or right held as a prerogative of status or rank, and exercised to the exclusion or detriment of others."

Having an advantage, special rights, status, rank and immunity I believe is a benefit we would all like to have. We might say, "Oh, if I become a Christian I will have to repent." No, the truth is not that we HAVE TO repent. The truth is that we GET TO repent, and also RECEIVE ETERNAL LIFE! Would anyone like to have this gift today? I do.

_____

_____

_____

_____

_____

_____

_____

_____

328

Our identity in Jesus, who are we, what is our position, where are we? He has given us wealth that is beyond $'s.

Ephesians 2:4-10 (NLT)

"But God is so rich in mercy, and he loved us so much, that even though we were dead because of our sins, he gave us life when he raised Christ from the dead. It is only by God's grace that you have been saved! For he raised us from the dead along with Christ and SEATED US with Him in the Heavenly realms because we are united with Christ Jesus. So God can point to us in all future ages as examples of the incredible WEALTH of his grace and kindness toward us, as shown in all He has done for us who are united with Christ Jesus.

God saved you by his grace when you believed. And you can't take credit for this; it is a gift from God. Salvation is not a reward for the good things we have done, so none of us can boast about it. For we are God's masterpiece. He has created us anew in Christ Jesus so we can do the good things he planned for us long ago."

Let us be the true people we really are today. If we have God's grace, then we are the richest people on this planet. Thank You Jesus.

_____

_____

_____

_____

_____

_____

_____

Acts 11:18 (NLT) "...We can see that God has also given the Gentiles the PRIVILEGE of REPENTING of their sins and receiving eternal life."

Yes, we all sin. A Christian, can see another Christian that is looked up to and think, "Surely, that person is not like me, stumbling and sinning about." Guess what? We're all alike. We can't boast of our salvation. Ephesians 2:9 (NLT) "Salvation is not a reward for the good things we have done. So none of us can boast about it." So, let's stop hiding our sin's out of shame. As Christians, repenting is not just something we have to do, but it is actually a PRIVILEGE. It is an honor to be able to do this. It also leads toward receiving ETERNAL LIFE. So, lets humble ourselves and receive this great honor and PRIVILEGE. "Confess your sins to one another and pray for one another so that you might be healed." James 5:16 (WEB)

330

TRIALS. We all have them. They are actually a GIFT that brings out God's best in us.

Check out Colossians 3:12-15 (NLT) " Since God chose you to be the holy people he loves, you must clothe yourselves with tenderhearted mercy, kindness, humility, gentleness, and patience. Make allowance for each other's faults, and forgive anyone who offends you. Remember, the Lord forgave you, so you must forgive others. Above all, clothe yourselves with love, which binds us all together in perfect harmony. And let the peace that comes from Christ rule in your hearts. For as members of one body you are called to live in peace. And always be thankful."

All of these qualities, characteristics, responses and actions are only needed when the opposite confronts us. So, let us be 'thankful' in all things and continue to allow the Holy Spirit to sharpen us into becoming more like Jesus.

So, thank God for that person in High School who offended me or that person who offended me a few weeks ago in church! I now have the PRIVILEGE to forgive and put into action the qualities of character that are from our merciful Lord Jesus.

331

Are we ready to let go, and ENTER? Colossians 3:3 (NLT) "For you died to this life, and your real life is hidden with Christ in God." Col 3:5 (NLT) "So put to death the sinful, earthly things lurking within you..." Col 3:10 (NLT)"Put on your new nature, and be renewed as you learn to know your Creator and become like him."

It's a journey! But first, we have to dive in! "Jesus, I accept You as my Lord and Savior. I believe You died for the forgiveness of my sins that I would receive eternal life with You. Send me your Holy Spirit that I may have Your Spirit inside me and be a new creation. Thank You Jesus. In Your name"

_____

_____

_____

_____

_____

_____

_____

_____

_____

_____

_____

_____

Simple words, Simple teaching, but so God POWERFUL, that it could set us free and be LIFE CHANGING now.

"Make allowance for each other's faults, and forgive anyone who offends you. Remember, the Lord forgave you, so you must forgive others."

Colossians 3:13 (NLT)

This is a key, given to us by God, to unlock the door keeping us from our freedom!

_____

_____

_____

_____

_____

_____

_____

_____

_____

_____

_____

_____

_____

_____

333

Today's hope to face our world: POWER. It is what God offers us.

1Corinthians 4:20 (NLT)

"For the Kingdom of God is not just a lot of talk; it is living by God's power."

334

How do we take on this world daily when we're experiencing such bombardment? Well, these are God's Words. Let's take them as a matter of fact and live by them.

1 John 4:4 (NLT)_ "...because the Spirit who lives in you is greater than the spirit who lives in the world."

_____

_____

_____

_____

_____

_____

_____

_____

_____

_____

_____

_____

_____

PRAY! There is a higher realm. There are principalities and powers of the darkness. Let us not forget that we are not called to just fight evil and protect with earthly powers, and weapons. We are called, # 1, to fight the enemy who hates God's people and Jerusalem, with a power greater than any nuclear bomb.

Acts 4:27-31 (NLT) " 'In fact, this has happened here in this very city! For Herod Antipas, Pontius Pilate, the governor, the Gentiles, and the people of Israel were all united against Jesus, your holy servant, whom you anointed. But, everything they did was determined beforehand according to your will. And now, O Lord, hear their threats, and give us, your servants, great boldness in preaching your word. Stretch out your hand with healing power; may miraculous signs and wonders be done through the name of your holy servant Jesus.'"

336

Let us pray for the Jews today, out of love, but not just for protection, but for salvation, that their eyes might be opened.

Romans 10:1-4 (NLT)

"Dear brothers and sisters, the longing of my heart and my prayer to God is for the people of Israel to be saved. I know what enthusiasm they have for God, but it is misdirected zeal. For they don't understand God's way of making people right with himself. Refusing to accept God's way, they cling to their own way of getting right with God by trying to keep the law. For Christ has already accomplished the purpose for which the law was given. As a result, all who believe in him are made right with God."

337

To become a champion of something it takes practice, right? How bout 'Loving each other with all our heart'? Maybe we should truly practice this today? Starting by coming to the Lord in prayer and asking Him to empower us by the Holy Spirit and change us. Then, let's 'hit the field!', and practice.

1 Peter 1:22,23 (NLT)"You were cleansed from your sins when you obeyed the truth, so now you must show sincere love to each other as brothers and sisters. LOVE EACH OTHER DEEPLY with ALL YOUR HEART for you have been BORN AGAIN, but not to a life that will quickly end. Your new life will last forever because it comes from the eternal, Living Word of God."

Romans 6:15 (NLT)

"Well then, since God's grace has set us free from the law, does that mean we can go on sinning? Of course not!.........."

"Now you must give yourselves to be slaves to righteous living so that you will become holy." Holiness is a process. It is a call upon our lives. He wouldn't call us to something we couldn't have. BE HOLY!!! And, REJOICE!!! It is all His gift!!! A gift is free. We don't pay for it. We show thankfulness!!! Grace is free!!! All from God, our Father, is

FREE!!! Do we want it?

_____

_____

_____

_____

_____

_____

_____

_____

_____

_____

_____

_____

339

I woke early this morning and felt I heard God saying He wanted to speak to me. Where it was coming from did not feel like my normal thought patterns. This is what I heard, and, I am thinking, maybe it is not just for me, but also for family and friends, "I SPEAK LIFE INTO YOU, NOT DEATH."

God created the heavens and the earth with His spoken Word. Where do we need these words spoken into our lives today? Let us, let Him, speak, and hear His words.

_____

_____

_____

_____

_____

_____

_____

_____

_____

_____

_____

_____

_____

340

Christ's cross. Let us embrace it, and run to it, and live by it. It is our source of power. What? Does that seem foolish? Please listen.

1 Corinthians 1:18-21 (NLT)

"The message of the Cross is foolishness for those headed to destruction! But we who are being saved know it is the very power of God. As the scriptures say,

'I will destroy the wisdom of the wise and discard the intelligence of the intelligent.'

So where does this leave the philosophers, the scholars, and the world's brilliant debaters? God has made the wisdom of this world look foolish. Since God in His wisdom saw to it that the world would never know Him through human wisdom, He has used our foolish preaching to save those who believe."

The CROSS. The SACRIFICE. The ALL. KNOW HIM.

_____

_____

_____

_____

_____

_____

_____

_____

_____

FOREVER. Though we may not see it as being a part of our lives yet, we live in it. Nothing can take it away from us.

1 Thessalonians 4:16-18 (NLT)

"For the Lord Himself will come down from heaven with a commanding shout, with the voice of the archangel, and with the trumpet call of God. First, the Christians who have died will rise from their graves. Then, together with them, we who are still alive and remain on this earth will be caught up in the clouds to meet the Lord in the air. Then we will be with the Lord FOREVER. So, encourage each other with these words."

Breathe it in now. We are a part of forever.

_____

_____

_____

_____

_____

_____

_____

_____

_____

_____

342

The Bible tells us to especially seek the gift of prophecy. It is the grand connector with the pulse, the channel, of the Almighty. It connects all parts of the body, His church, together in humility, unity, and power.

2 Peter 1:21 (NIV)

"For prophecy never had its origin in the human will, but prophets, though human, spoke from God as they were carried along by the Holy Spirit."

The Bible also says that we 'have not' because we don't ask. What is God saying? Does He want us to get aggressive in pursuing, 'His Kingdom come. His will be done.' Shall we sit today and let the world's worries, our own thoughts, wants, needs and pleasures, lead and guide us today, or shall we go into the Throne room of God to pray, ask, and receive from our loving Father today. We can be different! The Holy Spirit CAN change the way we think today. God has a mission for each one of us today. #1 Receive His LOVE. Yes, He LOVES US!

_____
_____
_____
_____
_____
_____
_____
_____
_____
_____

Getting a bit beat up lately in any realm of our humanity? We see the natural realm and decipher that which we see based upon natural human learning. Yet, the Bible says we live in a supernatural realm, a realm of evil principalities and powers in the high places. In the authority, the name of Jesus, we are to do warfare and move this enemies meddling out of others and our own lives. What we don't see is the norm, and, whether we like it or not, we are in this spiritual reality world. So, we must learn to take the authority of Jesus and fight. Acts 16:18 (NLT) "This went on day after day until Paul got so exasperated that he turned and said to the demon within her, 'I command you in the name of Jesus Christ to come out of her.' And instantly it left her." What an awesome powerful God we serve.

_____

_____

_____

_____

_____

_____

_____

_____

_____

_____

_____

_____

_____

How do I get powered up today with a new mind to freely live and freely love others? How do we truly learn to live in God's freedom and power over sin? Is it following the law or is it through grace?

Romans 6:14 (NLT)

"Sin is no longer your master, for you NO LONGER live under the requirements of the law. Instead, you live under the freedom of God's grace."

Rom 6:23 (NLT)

"For the wages of sin is death, but the FREE gift of God is eternal life through Christ Jesus our Lord." GRACE-Receiving something we don't deserve is obviously free. Be free in your life today! The enemy hates this.

_____
_____
_____
_____
_____
_____
_____
_____
_____
_____

345

Do not forget our identity. Even though we have fallen we can still step, it still is a simple, though seemingly complicated, step into the light. There is light ahead!

1 Peter 2:9 (NIV)

"But you are a chosen people, a royal priesthood, a holy nation, God's special possession, that you may declare the praises of him who called you out of darkness into his wonderful light."

—————————————————————————
—————————————————————————
—————————————————————————
—————————————————————————
—————————————————————————
—————————————————————————
—————————————————————————
—————————————————————————
—————————————————————————
—————————————————————————
—————————————————————————
—————————————————————————
—————————————————————————

346

Surely, we know that Christ is among us? Test and examine ourselves. Are we really Christians?

2 Corinthians 13:5 (NLT)

"Examine yourselves to see if your faith is genuine. Test yourselves. Surely you know that Jesus Christ is among you; if not, you have failed the test of genuine faith."

The Life Application Study Bible's notes on this verse help to see what this testing is for. "Just as we get physical checkups, Paul urges us to give ourselves spiritual checkups. We should look for a growing awareness of Christ's presence and power in our life. Then we will know if we are true Christians or merely impostors. If we are not actively seeking to grow closer to God, we are drawing further away from Him."

_____

_____

_____

_____

_____

_____

_____

_____

_____

_____

347

What has God given us? God has given us something very powerful, the FREEDOM OF CHOICE. He has laid a plate out before us, an easel, clay on a pottery wheel. What we do with our life, how we choose to live our life is up to us. We don't always get the choice of what we receive, but we do have the choice of how we will ultimately respond and how we will allow God to be a part and make something beautiful out of it.

Here is Paul's final word's in 2 Corinthians 13:11 (NLT)

"Dear brothers and sisters, I close my letter with these last words: Be joyful. Grow to maturity. Encourage each other. Live in harmony and peace. Then the God of love and peace will be with you."

Paul tells the people, including us, to live like this because we can. We have the choice. So, when the plate is put before us, even though an item may be difficult, we still have our freedom to allow God to work His wonders through it. We ARE HIS WORK OF BEAUTY if we but ALLOW. He is with us. He is for us. His love for us is beyond our human comprehension. Grace and peace.

348

Psalm 23:4 (NIV)

"Even though I walk through the darkest valley, I will fear no evil, for you are with me; your rod and your staff, they comfort me."

Picture yourself going through the darkest valley with no army with you, only yourself, and wild beasts around you. Picture this, and trusting without fear that God is with you and will protect. Now, let us go to the reality of the world we live in and do the same.

_____

_____

_____

_____

_____

_____

_____

_____

_____

_____

_____

_____

STAND FIRM. "Stand firm and you will see the deliverance of the Lord." The Lord will do the miraculous to deliver. Our part in this, in the midst, while the enemy, or the attack still seems present, is to STAND FIRM and hear our Father's Words.

Exodus 14:13 (NIV)

13 Moses answered the people, "Do not be afraid. Stand firm and you will see the deliverance the LORD will bring you today. The Egyptians you see today you will never see again."

STAND FIRM

_____

_____

_____

_____

_____

_____

_____

_____

_____

_____

_____

_____

_____

350

Colossians 3:15 (NIV)

"15 Let the peace of Christ rule in your hearts, since as members of one body you were called to peace. And be thankful."

I can't do this! No matter how hard I try, I can't have this peace in my mind.

There is a difference between trying, ourselves, to generate His peace in our lives, and actually ALLOWING or LETTING His peace to rule in our hearts and minds. The later refers to a surrender, a yielding from our own efforts, and permitting Him to do something in our minds and hearts He is already giving to us. He is actively giving it to us. We need to actively let Him. It is there for the taking. We need to 'let go' of our attempts to produce or control. His love for us is so deep. Let us grasp and hold onto at least a portion of it as it flows through our bodies today. Be thankful. His love for each of us is immense.

_____

_____

_____

_____

_____

_____

_____

_____

_____

351

I speak truth! Truth sets us free! It is not my truth. It is His truth! With everything He has done and given us we must choose to get up off our ground and walk in His glory! He has given us THE KINGDOM! Let's walk in it!!!

1 Thessalonians 2:12 (NLT)

"We pleaded with you, encouraged you, and urged you to live your lives in a way that God would consider worthy. For he called you to share in his Kingdom and glory."

Yes, He called His children to share in HIS GLORY.

_____

_____

_____

_____

_____

_____

_____

_____

_____

_____

_____

_____

_____

352

Can we COMPLETELY trust in Jesus today so that there is not ONE worry. Go ahead, make each of those worries an offering and prayer to Jesus. Now trust Him COMPLETELY.

Romans 15:13 (NIV)

13 May the God of hope fill you with all joy and peace as you trust in him, so that you may overflow with hope by the power of the Holy Spirit

_____

_____

_____

_____

_____

_____

_____

_____

_____

_____

_____

_____

_____

353

Please listen! Believers and non-believers!

Galatians 5:4-6 (NLT)

"For if you are trying to make yourselves right with God by keeping the law, you have been cut off from Christ! You have fallen away from God's grace.

But we who live by the Spirit eagerly await to receive the righteousness God has promised to us. For when we place our faith in Christ Jesus, there is no benefit in being circumcised or being uncircumcised. What is important is FAITH expressing itself in LOVE."

Quickly turn the page and experience and see that it is by receiving God's love that we are changed. It is not by changing first that we receive His love. He is the 'LIFTER of our heads'. So, let us walk with our heads lifted high today through whatever we are presented in life.

_____

_____

_____

_____

_____

_____

_____

_____

_____

_____

Hey! He said it first!

"Become Holy!" Think about that as we number our days.

Romans 6:19 (NLT) "...Now you must give yourselves to be slaves to righteous living so that you will become HOLY."

_____

_____

_____

_____

_____

_____

_____

_____

_____

_____

_____

_____

_____

355

Romans 8:3 (NLT)

"He sent His own Son in a body like the bodies we sinners have..." Imagine God, all of a sudden, experiencing a new location life and existing in a human body. We too, will be experiencing, all of a sudden, existing in a new location and a heavenly body. Can we see it? Look! It's in us now! We will see it! Let us take heart! Be bold, be brave, For the Lord our God is with us!

356

Let's understand and live by a key ingredient in our faith in Christ.

Romans 11:22 (NLT)

"Notice how God is both kind and severe. He is severe to those who disobeyed, but kind to you if you continue to trust in His kindness." Do not let it become a matter of your works that get you God's approval. We've already got it because of His death on the cross before we could even do one good work. Did the sinner dying on the cross have time to come off the cross and do some good works before he received Jesus' promise, Luke 23:43 (NLT) "Today you will be with me in paradise!" We must see and believe that salvation is by God's kindness. If you've never simply asked Jesus to save you, please ask Him today. We are saved by His kindness.

_____

_____

_____

_____

_____

_____

_____

_____

_____

_____

_____

357

PEACE! PEACE! PEACE! Out of this world, but in this world, REAL PEACE! Peace in your mind! Peace in your soul! Peace in every breath you take! This is what Jesus came to give us. Ask and it is yours.

EPHESIANS 2:17 (NLT)

"He brought this Good News of peace to you Gentiles, who were far away from him, and peace to the Jews who were near. Now all of us can come to the Father through the same Holy Spirit because of what Christ has done for us."

Let's breathe in His peace today. It is even greater today than any current world battles.

PEACE!

_____

_____

_____

_____

_____

_____

_____

_____

_____

_____

_____

358

POWERFUL are our prayers!!! God is All-Powerful but He has chosen to let us help Him change the world, and people's lives, through our prayers. We do not understand it all. How holy and cherished by God are our prayers. Revelations says our prayers are incense before God's throne.

1 Timothy 2-6 (NLT)

"... I urge you, first of all, to pray for all people. ask God to help them; intercede on their behalf, and give thanks for them.... For there is One God and One Mediator who can reconcile God and humanity--the man Christ Jesus. He gave his life to purchase freedom for everyone."

Let us not forget the POWER of our prayers today.

359

Paul's desires for the Colossian church:

Colossians 2:2 (NLT)

"I want them to be encouraged and knit together by strong ties of love."

How can we have, or experience, this love if we don't have close community, and God's family, His blood brothers and sisters, that we give and receive from? God's command, "Do not forsake the gathering." makes sense. We need strong loving family that is connected to the Almighty. "STRONG TIES OF LOVE."

We all need them. Father in heaven, send Your love to all those I know today.

_____

_____

_____

_____

_____

_____

_____

_____

_____

_____

360

Let us not think of God's Word as a mere add on to our lives. It is not secondary to our other needs in life. Rather, it is our very breath of life. It is alive and working in us. For He has called us to share in His Kingdom and glory. This is an offer that overwhelms any offer this world presents.

1Thessalonians 2:12 (NLT)

"We pleaded with you, encouraged you, and urged you to live your lives in a way that God would consider WORTHY. For He called you to SHARE in his Kingdom and GLORY."

_____

_____

_____

_____

_____

_____

_____

_____

_____

_____

_____

_____

361

Tears came to my eyes today while thinking on how powerful our prayers actually are. God loves to hear them. They are incense before His thrown. Is He teasing us when He says 'Never stop praying'? No! He will act! But He will act according to His heavenly desires, not our earthly desires and earthly wisdom. Thank God for that. We pray for our immediate family. But, what struck me today was to also pray for the chain of our brothers and sisters family and their children. Also, to pray for those individuals that God brought across our past path's that would come to mind. How glorious! It makes a difference!

1 Thessalonians 5:16-18 (NLT)

"Always be joyful. NEVER stop praying. Be thankful in all circumstances, for this is God's will for you who belong to Christ Jesus."

_____

_____

_____

_____

_____

_____

_____

_____

_____

_____

_____

What holiday is coming up? Thanksgiving!! What a time to be thankful for the greatest gift God has given us! GRACE! Yes, He has forgiven our sins! And, if you haven't experienced this yet, all you got to do is ask Him. How glorious! Now we can go dance in the rain shouting for joy, "Jesus is King!!"

2 Corinthians 4:15 (NLT)

15 All this is for your benefit, so that the GRACE that is reaching more and more people may cause THANKSGIVING to overflow to the glory of God.

_____

_____

_____

_____

_____

_____

_____

_____

_____

_____

_____

363

Hey, yo! There is absolutely no condemnation in Christ. If we really want to change our actions or thoughts, our sinful ways, we are struggling with, let us stop, with our own strength, in trying harder to overcome so that we may be acceptable or approved by Him. Let us listen to Him instead as He says, "If you really want to change then come sit in my presence. You are welcome here, and I will change you."

364

Revelation 1:3 (NLT) "God blesses the one who reads the words of the prophecy to the church, and he blesses all who listen to its message and obey what it says, for the TIME IS NEAR."

Happy Thanksgiving all!!! Yes, the world and our country have serious trials. Yet, the Lord ultimately rules. Let us give thanksgiving for that. Also, thanksgiving for today, that we are able, in peace, to come together with our God given, loved families and celebrate God's goodness, love and mercies He has given us. Let us thank Him for the peace today and remember that, "THE TIME IS NEAR."

365

Just do it! There is glory and victory in this! He has already paid the price for us to enter the courts of His amazing place. Yes, on our own merits we are not worthy. So, no need for us to hesitate! Regardless of our stumbles and falls, we are approved to enter! This is where we are changed!

Psalms 100:4 (NIV)

"Enter his gates with thanksgiving and his courts with praise; give thanks to him and praise his name."

_____

_____

_____

_____

_____

_____

_____

_____

_____

_____

_____

_____

366

We need a supernatural cleansing; a knowing of our supernatural identity and what is our destination. These are provided by our Heavenly Father, our Savior Jesus.

John 13:1-5 (NLT)"Before the Passover celebration, Jesus knew that his hour had come to leave this world and RETURN to his FATHER. He had loved his disciples during his ministry on earth, and now he loved them to the very end. It was time for supper, and the devil had already prompted Judas, Son of Simon Iscariot, to betray Jesus. Jesus knew that the Father had given him authority over everything and that he had come from God and would return to God. So he got up from the table, took off his robe wrapped a towel around his waist, and poured water into a Basin. Then he began to wash the disciple's feet, drying them with the towel he had around him."

JESUS knew he would be betrayed, even by those he loved. He knows His authority also and His destination. Then, even with His knowledge of betrayal he still loves and serves them. This is Supernatural love, and this is the love He has called us to have also. SUPERNATURAL!!! His love! Why, how!? Because He lives within us.

367

Whatever trials we are going through here is God's word to us: 2 Peter 3:18 (NLT)

"Rather, you must grow in the GRACE and KNOWLEDGE of our Lord and Savior Jesus Christ. All glory to Him, both now and forever! Amen."

_____

_____

_____

_____

_____

_____

_____

_____

_____

_____

_____

_____

_____

_____

_____

Now this is your message space. God is speaking to all of us! The journey continues. Ask for, and allow Him to, and the Holy Spirit will come and speak to us and even change the way we think. Open His Word, and He will open the eyes of our hearts. God loves His children so much. My prayer for us is that we are open to the Lord's love and that we hear the Father's loving voice. May this be done in Jesus name. Amen.

_____

_____

_____

_____

_____

_____

_____

_____

_____

_____

_____

_____

_____

_____

Printed in the United States
by Baker & Taylor Publisher Services